*The Survival
Handbook*

The Survival Handbook

W. K. MERRILL

AN
ARC
BOOK

ARCO PUBLISHING COMPANY, INC.
219 Park Avenue South, New York, N.Y. 10003

An ARC Book

Published 1974 by Arco Publishing Company, Inc.
219 Park Avenue South, New York, N.Y. 10003
by arrangement with Winchester Press

Library of Congress Catalog Card Number 73-88649
ISBN 0-668-03345-2

Printed in the United States of America

DEDICATION

To the Rangers, State Game and Fire Wardens, Fire Department Rescue Units, Sheriff's Rescue Squads, State Police, Royal Canadian Mounted Police, United States and Royal Canadian Coast Guard, Air-Sea Rescue Units of the Army, Navy, and Marine Corps, Doctors and Para-medic Teams, Ski Patrolmen, and those unsung heroes, the Mountain Rescue Associations and organizations made up of private citizens who risk their lives and give freely of their time without compensation—and to my lifelong friend Edi Jaun

Contents

1

Introduction

You are backpacking on the Appalachian Trail. You are enjoying the freedom the wilderness has in large amount. You have the hiking equipment you need, and nothing else. The whole point of the trip was to leave behind the cumbersome world and its possessions.

Right?

Then, why do you need to know about survival and all the techniques involved in such a terror-ridden word?

Simply because in the outdoors emergencies arise. Trouble cannot always be avoided. Even though you may not be planning to run away from home to try to make it the primitive way in the wilderness, you may find yourself unexpectedly in a survival situation.

Things happen.

On a simple one-day fishing or camping trip you could get turned around and lose your way. How do you cope? There are proven methods of finding your way without map or compass (of course, you should have both, in which case there are other methods). See Chapters 2 and 3.

Sudden Indian summer snowstorms do occur in the Idaho wilds and in the Grand Tetons; you may be stranded there.

During a rain squall in the woods you may become disoriented and lost in strange terrain. If you had a choice, would you rather catch pneumonia or have a snug nest made from boughs and a sheltered fire while you waited for dawn when you could reorient yourself and find the way back to camp?

Although there are many horror stories of people perishing a few miles from civilization, the chances are you will only experience a few hours or, perhaps, a day or two of discomfort, disorder and the gripping fear of the unknown—if you are prepared.

Your forefathers, the men who mapped this country, who searched for and found the mountain passes, who blazed trails through the woods and fought the desert, survived, and even thrived, under what today we consider emergency conditions. What was everyday living to them can be adventure for you. Becoming lost or even being shipwrecked is nobody's idea of fun, but even a plane crash can be turned into nothing more than an adventure if you are prepared.

Also, quite apart from the emergency situation, good survival technique—the knowledge of how to live comfortably far from the local hardware, grocery and gasoline station—adds to your enjoyment of the woods, the mountains or the ocean. It is another layer of knowledge as necessary as an insulated set of underwear in the Arctic.

This is why I have gathered together these bits and pieces of information on all kinds of lore, for all kinds of climate conditions, for all types of terrain.

During my 36 ranger years I experienced different

Survival situations can be nothing more than adventures,
if you have the proper know-how.

survival situations in different areas. I have tried to include in this book information on almost every possible situation you might encounter so that, should an emergency occur, you cannot only survive, but do it in style and with a certain degree of comfort. And you'll have the emotional comfort of knowing what to do.

I have even included rather involved information on stalking prey, keeping meat fresh, jungle lore, and building elaborate snow shelters for cold climates. Even if you happen to want to be a nature boy or do a Robinson Crusoe, you'll have to know how to build your own tree house.

Needless to say, no one should venture from the highways without basic safety equipment. I won't even call this survival equipment. It's too elementary.

You should not go into the wilderness without a knife, a metal match or cigarette lighter, a compass and map, a plastic tarp, a small first aid kit and a large orange colored handkerchief for signaling. An ideal piece of equipment would combine several of these, for example, a poncho/tarp of brilliant color.

These essentials can easily be carried in the pockets of your jacket or in your knapsack. They don't constitute a survival kit. But they are as necessary as good hiking boots or life jackets on a boat.

This book will fit into your knapsack. And, hopefully, you will take it along. But even if it is on your library shelf while you are on a plane that crashes in the back-country, or on a boat that catches fire and sinks, or lost in the woods or in any situation that calls for survival knowledge you should be able mentally to thumb through this book and find the advice you need.

Preparedness is the key to survival. The Boy Scout slogan is just as true today as it always was.

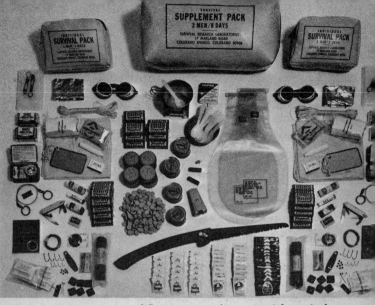

There are many different types of commercial survival kits. Other do-it-yourself varieties are explained throughout the book.

Take some possible situations. You are camping in the High Sierra and a summer storm with lightning and heavy rain occurs with little warning. You become lost when you scurry to get away from the heavy trees and find an open place to stand. The storm passes. It's night, but you don't know which way to go to find your way back to camp. There are bears in the woods around you. What should you do? The chapter on Orienting Yourself will tell you.

You are vacationing off the Florida Keys and the commercial fishing boat you are on for the day catches fire. You must abandon ship. Do you even know the correct way to jump into the sea? The chapter on Water Survival will help you here.

You are on a flight from San Francisco to Norway,

via the polar route. The plane crashes and you are stranded on polar ice. Can you survive? Yes. If you've read the section on Cold Weather Survival.

Of course, during World War II, adventures such as we are talking about happened frequently. Men crashed on tiny Aleutian islands and survived months alone in

A lost hiker, properly equipped for emergencies, enjoys his solitude while awaiting rescue.

the Arctic climate. A group of Japanese soldiers living in the jungle of the Philippine islands were so isolated that they were not discovered until five years after World War II had ended.

The Flying Tigers shot down in China fought their way across mountains, through the Burmese jungle to reach villages where they lived and gained strength to struggle on through the jungle to reach their base.

These men are not the famous names of American history. They weren't the Kit Carsons and Captain John Fremonts or John Colters. They were men who survived incredible odds—and not so long ago either.

Their successes depended on equal units of resourcefulness and bravery. Both are qualities you must have in abundance if you are going to venture off city pavements. But they had know-how as well. They had been taught the basic fundamentals of survival, the same techniques I have written here.

Naturally, when you go camping or backpacking, or sailing, you hope and expect to avoid trouble. So you carry the items I mentioned above as a matter of course. You have your first aid kit, your knife, your lighter, your signal scarf, a compass and map. And you have read the chapters in this book so you know how to find your way back to camp, you can signal a rescue plane properly, you can do what has to be done in the circumstances to avoid further trouble. You can handle yourself well if an emergency does arise because you have some know-how.

There are right and wrong things to do when an emergency arises, and you've learned the right things to do—and how to avoid the wrong ones.

It all begins before you start out. You take out success insurance by planning ahead. Where are you going?

What will you need? What problems could you encounter?

You can use this simple check list to avoid some trouble:

1. Check the weather reports.

   You don't want to hike in a heavy downpour or into a snowstorm. Small craft warnings posted by the Coast Guard mean just that.

In Inyo National Forest, hikers at the 14,000-foot Sierra divide at the Palisades Glaciers.

2. Take out your maps or charts and study them so you'll have a picture of the terrain you are going into.

3. Check all equipment before you load it for the trip. A broken knapsack strap, an incomplete first aid kit or canteens with holes can turn your weekend into an endurance test.

4. Be certain the people traveling with you are healthy.

5. Be certain your vehicle is as healthy as the people in it. Have your jeep thoroughly checked out. A vapor lock in the desert can create an instant survival situation. And a blow-out on a mountain road may be a movie stunt man's idea of fun, but not what you need. Double-check the tires. They are important.

This simple list seems self-evident. But it's the start of your insurance for a successful trip.

And about that first aid kit.

Don't rush out to buy a kit of items someone else has decided you need. Think of the accidents that could befall *you*. Are there mosquitoes where you are going? Could someone walk into poison ivy? What did you need the last time you were hiking?

Here's a list of some of the essentials for a first aid kit. Use this as a guide and add to it or subtract from it as you think necessary.

insect repellent
aspirin
iodine
adhesive bandages
gauze pads and adhesive tape
tweezers (for splinters)

ointment for burns
calamine lotion
sunburn lotion or oil
small bar of soap (save the kind you get in motels)
folding cup
water purification tablets
seasickness pills
extra pair of socks
first aid guide

You've done everything you could think of to avoid trouble. You prepared as well as you could. And trouble came and found you. You are suddenly in the middle of a disaster situation.

This is not what you anticipated. Here's what to do.

Fight down your panic. Stay as calm as you can. Calm other members of your group. Fear can be an obstacle to your well-being as ominous as an angry bear. Look your situation over as calmly as possible. You can't afford to be fearful or hysterical. There are certain decisions you must make now.

Appraise the situation. You have to take inventory of your plight and weigh your alternatives.

Have you or anyone else been injured? If you are hurt you probably should remain where you are and signal for help even before looking for food or water. The chapter on Signaling will tell you what to do and how to do it. Remember, most wilderness is constantly surveyed by planes or spotters in towers. Someone will see you. But without the proper signal, a plane might think you are a lone camper waving hello—not a man in distress.

Have you crashed? Aircraft rescue search is generally thorough and swift. A downed plane can be seen more easily than a lone survivor. You would be better off staying with the plane.

Now you must orient yourself to find out where you are in relation to what you know. Where is your base camp? How far away is your jeep? Was that mountain always in front of you? You must decide if you should stay where you are or attempt to rescue yourself. What chance do you have of finding your way out? Are you reasonably close to civilization? Which direction is it? How great a risk would you take if you decided to walk out? Can you live for days or weeks where you are? The chapter on Orienting Yourself will help you here.

Coast Guard boats fighting fire on the training ship Aquamaut II, near Plum Island, Mass.

In this handbook I've tried to anticipate all possible situations you might encounter. The help you need is right in your hand.

There is a chapter on Woodlore, which will certainly enhance your enjoyment of the outdoors, even if you don't need it to survive. You might never want to go home after you've caught that partridge and roasted it over a fire you built beside your cozy tree bough shelter.

Another thing to remember if you are in a strange part of the world is that someone calls it home.

If you are lost in the desert, it may seem as if only the lizards like it. But the Pueblo and Digger Indians live there. In the chapter on Desert Survival, you'll learn how to catch water in a solar still, how to find food, how to build a shelter to protect you from the desert chill, and how to find your way out.

The chapter on Cold Weather doesn't mention the Eskimos, but they do live there all year round. I have advice on how to protect yourself from the cold, how to build a shelter and find food. Water is readily available. It needs only melting; and I explain how to build a fire in the snow.

There's a chapter on living the way the Swiss Family Robinson did on an island, in case you are shipwrecked, and how to survive in a jungle where the food is plentiful, but survival requires special techniques.

Should you be caught in the mountains, there is a chapter that might remind you that mountaineering was a way of life for the Hudson Bay Company trappers.

There are a few general cautions you must take no matter what your terrain.

Do not drink water the first day if your water is limited. You probably do not need water and it will be wasted.

Do not drink sea water under any circumstances.

Do not eat meat, fish, wild fowl, fats, proteins or dehydrated foods if you do not have sufficient water in your system for proper digestion. They will make you very ill.

Do not eat uncooked animal meat.

Do not be careless in making an emergency camp. Select your bed and site carefully. Shake out all clothing, boots, hat and bedding. There might be a poisonous spider, snake or scorpion hiding inside.

Do not stay on a high ridge during a storm. Drop to a lower elevation to avoid possible lightning strikes, high wind and cold. Seek shelter in a cave or under an overhanging rock.

Do not stay near timber in a high wind. Timber can be a widow-maker. If you are in a forest, stand or sit close to a large rock.

One final word: no matter what kind of terrain you are in or how bad it may look at the moment, in any survival situation, remember, if you have the know-how, nature will provide.

And the know-how is in the following pages.

2

Map Reading and Compass Use

Too little is said in manuals and outdoor handbooks about that small but important gadget, the compass and its companion, the map. Everyone who enters unfamiliar wilderness country needs a map and a compass.

It must be remembered that no person is born with the innate ability to find his way into and back out of unfamiliar wilderness country. This prowess is acquired by learning and observing the surrounding terrain, and by using a good compass. A good contour map is also a necessity. These two important items complement each other like ham and eggs.

Survival experts and rescue organizations say that thousands of people who get lost in our recreational areas each year would remain oriented if they carried a compass and map and knew how to use them properly.

For the offshore fisherman, a navigation chart of the waters he will be in is a *must!* The chart (marine map) complements the marine compass and gives information needed for a safe return to shore: compass variation, depths, lights, channels, buoys, etc. Currents are shown on separate charts. The new small craft boating charts are compact and give compass courses to run (and reverse courses), marinas and supply points, anchorages and shoreside facilities.

What Maps Can Do for You

Reading a map requires some thought and study. A map is a printed picture of the land as seen from above; maps are street signs of the wilderness. Study them before a trip. After you are lost, it is too late to practice how to interpret your map or use your compass!

Topographical maps will give you the declination (variation) for the area you are in—scale, section, range, township, elevations, roads, trails, streams, rivers, peaks and a host of other valuable data. By orienting your map with a compass or the terrain, as described in Chapter 3, you can lay out a compass course and reach any place shown on the map. With a little woods lore, you should have no fear about traveling through strange territory if you are observant and know how to use a map and compass.

Outdoorsmen respect the outdoors, but do not fear it. So practice the art of map reading and run compass courses near home before you take off for the woods or mountains.

Kinds of Maps

Maps are available in many scales and sizes and for many different uses. The most common type is a planimetric map, which shows all the land features such as roads, trails, rivers, etc. However, this type of map is best used to travel from the city to the general camping area; it does not have enough detail for wilderness travel.

For the camper or other sportsman who plans to travel on trails cross-country, a *topographical contour* map is best. This map shows all the features of the planimetric map, plus land shapes and elevation. The shape of the land is portrayed by imaginary lines following the ground surface at constant elevations above sea level. Topographical maps are colored to distinguish man-made and other features with date of survey, scale and declination noted.

Map Symbols

The illustrations here show the main symbols you will find on your map. In most maps the man-made features are colored black; the water features are colored blue; the vegetation features are colored green; and the elevation features are colored brown.

Here is a simple demonstration of contour lines: Dip rock part-way in water, draw water line. Dip one inch deeper, draw another line. Continue this process until the rock is completely wet. View from above.

Single track railroad . . . .

Multiple main line track railroad . . . .

Buildings (barn, warehouse, etc.) . . . .

Buildings (dwelling, place of employment)

School . . . .

Church . . . .

Cemetery . . . .   [†]   [Cem]

Telephone, telegraph, pipe line, etc. . . . . . .

Power transmission line . . . .

Open pit or quarry . . . .

Map symbols for man-made features are colored black.

Lake or pond........................... blue tint

Perennial streams ....

Spring ....

Water well ....

Marsh or swamp......................

Map symbols for water features are colored blue.

Most of the map symbols are self-evident. The contour lines, however, could use some explanation. A contour line indicates the height of the land above sea level. On your map, you'll notice that every fifth line is heavier than the surrounding lines. This is the line numbered to indicate height above sea level. These heavier lines are generally twenty feet apart, and the distance between them is called the contour interval. There is usually a note on the bottom of the map indicating the number of feet in the contour interval.

If you study the contour lines, you will see how they

Index contour .... ─────────

Intermediate contour .... ─────────

Depression contours ....

Cut ....

Fill ....

Large earth dam or levee ....

Sand area, sand dunes ....

Triangulation or transit traverse station .... △
   monumented with spirit level elev. .... BM△1062
Monumented bench mark, spirit level elev. ..... BM×958

Map symbols for elevation features are colored brown.

show a cliff when the lines run together; or a gentle slope with the lines far apart; and a mountaintop, where the line is a small circle. See the accompanying illustration.

Closed circles also indicate depressions, so one must note the nearby contour reading for accurate interpretation of an area's appearance.

Range Lines

Range lines seen marked at the top and bottom of topographic maps are laid off after townships have been established. They mark the east and west boundaries of townships. The six-mile strip of country between them is known as a "range," and is numbered east or west from the principal meridian from which the survey was made.

Direction Finding

Have you awakened in a strange area to find that you are "turned around?" The sun rises in the east and sets in the west regardless of your first impressions. Stand with your right hand to the morning sun or with your left hand to the evening sun and you will face approximately north. When you arrive in new country, look around, study the land masses and fix the directions well in your mind. When moving through new country, continue the practice of fixing direction and of looking all around you. A slow, careful trip will assure a sure and safe return.

Use of the Compass

A good compass (one with a protected face is best) is a must for traveling in strange country.

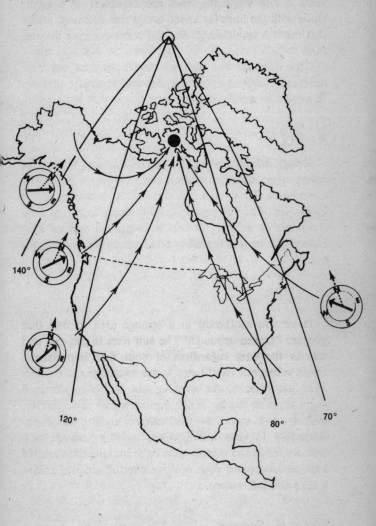

True north is the map direction toward the geographic North Pole; magnetic north is the compass direction toward the magnetic North Pole.

Check it out at the same time you are making your mental notes of direction and prominent land features. To orient the compass, hold it horizontally so that the needle swings freely. Avoid orienting your compass near any iron or steel as these will cause swinging of the needle and incorrect readings. When the needle on the dial comes to rest, rotate the compass so that the needle on the dial and north on the map coincide. Remember that this direction is magnetic north and may vary from true north by an appreciable degree. You must compute your declination variation for an accurate compass course.

Declination

Variation is represented on the map by lines connecting points of equal variation and is expressed in degrees east or west of a *baseline* where the declination variation is zero.

If you are east of this baseline, your compass will point west of true north.

If you are west of it, your compass needle will point east of true north. The declination is the angle difference between true north and magnetic north.

The variation of any point is indicated on your contour map. For example, if you are in an area where variation is 10° east, your compass will point east of true north. Therefore, if you now want to travel due north or 360° from where you are and maintain this direction, you must follow a heading of 350° (360° minus 10°) on your magnetic compass. In other words you travel 10° left or west of magnetic north. If you are, for instance, 10° west of true north on a course of 350° and want to travel true north, you would in this case have to add 10° to enable you to travel 360° or true course.

Here is a little rhyme that will be helpful:

East is least, *subtract* variation;
West is best, *add* variation.

Compass Readings

When you spread out your map, you will see a small triangle in the bottom margin. This is the declination, the angle between true north and the magnetic north field of the map, and of your compass.

To practice finding direction, spread out your map and draw a longitudinal line from one number at the top of the map to the corresponding number at the bottom of the map. This line from the north to the south number is called a meridian.

Now, on this meridian line, pick out one specific point and make that your base camp. Draw a straight line across the map through your base camp point.

In determining directions you must remember that any place *above* the camp on the meridian line is north, and any place *below* the camp on the meridian line is south. So it follows, any place on the straight line *left* of your camp is west and any place on the straight line *right* of your camp is east.

The illustrations here will show you how you can determine points like north-northeast and south-southwest.

The direction

northeast is halfway between east and north.
southeast is halfway between south and east.
southwest is halfway between south and west.
northwest is halfway between north and west.

That's pretty obvious.

Similarly, directions like north-northwest are merely

smaller slices of northwest. North-northwest is closer to north than west-northwest is. WNW is closer to west than to north.

Once you have mastered the idea of the sixteen different major pie slices that make up your compass, you are ready to use a protractor, an instrument used for measuring angles for more accurate readings. The protractor is a circle marked in 360 degrees, although some protractors are only half-circles for ease in carrying.

On the protractor, 0-360 is north, 180 is south, 90 is east and 270 is west.

Thus:

N—0 and 360	NNE—22½	NE—45	ENE—67½
E—90	ESE—112½	SE—135	SSE—157½
S—180	SSW—202½	SW—225	WSW—247½
W—270	WNW—292½	NW—315	NNW—337½

To learn the degrees in which you must travel to reach a specific point, center your protractor on your base camp. The north-south line on your map should line up with the protractor's 360-180 reading. Pick out a place where you wish to go. Now, merely look at the degree reading on the protractor at the edge of the protractor's circle. That's the number of degrees you must walk.

Traveling by Compass and Map

To hike from place to place outdoors you must set a course to follow. This is how you do it:

1. Stretch out your map and set your compass on the map with one long edge of its base plate touching both your starting point and your destination, with the base plate's arrow pointing to where you want

to go. The compass needle is not important at this point. It doesn't matter where it points.

2. Holding the base plate so that it touches your starting point and your destination, turn the compass housing so the orienting arrow lies parallel to the magnetic north line on your map. By using the magnetic north line you have automatically compensated for any compass declination on the route.

3. To travel to your destination, hold the compass before you at waist height with the direction of travel arrow pointing straight ahead of you. Turn yourself until the compass needle lies over the orienting arrow on the compass housing, with the north end of the needle pointing to the N on the housing. The direction of travel arrow now points to your destination.

You are ready to start out.

Setting a Course

To find out the number of degrees you should travel to reach a specific base from a specific point, you have to navigate. Here your protractor will help you.

Place your protractor-compass (the plate under most compasses has been designed as a protractor) on your map so that one edge of the base plate touches both your starting point and your destination. See the illustration. Your direction-of-travel arrow should point in the direction of your destination.

Now, turn the compass with its 360 degree markings until the orienting arrow points to north on the map. It must lie parallel to the nearest north-south meridian line with the arrow point toward north.

This is known as setting your compass. To find the direction you should take to reach your destination, look at the degree marking on the rim of the compass where the direction line touches it. There is your direction in degrees, or your bearing.

How to Offset Obstacles

In the "backcountry" it is almost impossible to travel a straight compass course due to rough terrain, such as large brush fields, swamps, lakes, canyons and other obstacles that force you to detour around them.

However, you can detour around them and get back on your compass course again by turning 90 degrees to the right or left of the obstacle, generally traveling the

The good hiker picks the most efficient route. Left: *strike for a landmark such as a lake shore to get closer to your destination; then go by compass from there.* Right: *Instead of climbing mountain, aim for bridge and follow roads. The most direct route may be all right for the crow to fly, but for the grounded hiker, it pays to examine the alternatives.*

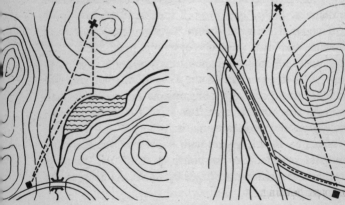

narrowest stretch. When you do make a 90-degree turn, you *must* count the number of steps you take to clear the obstacle. When this has been accomplished, turn right or left as the case calls for and continue on your primary course until the obstacle is cleared. Make another 90-degree turn, taking the same number of steps down the other side of the obstacle. This will bring you to your primary course again. To be certain, you should take a backsight and a foresight with your compass.

You may have to step a little off to one side or the other to get back exactly on line again.

Using the Compass as a Map

If you are standing on an elevated point and intend to travel to another elevated spot, you can take your bearing with your compass simply by holding it in your hand, turning the compass until the north compass needle rests over the north marking on the compass housing. Now, sight across the center of the compass and read the number of degrees on the compass housing opposite your face. This is the direction of the landmark in degrees.

If you start to walk toward that landmark using the bearing, and it is suddenly obscured from your view, you must fly blind at this point and use only your compass to locate your landmark. Say the bearing you had was 200 degrees. Hold your compass in your hand with the compass housing turned so its 200° marking is directly opposite your face, on the other side of the compass center. Rotate your whole body until you have the compass oriented so the north part of the compass needle rests pointing at the 360° north marking of the compass housing.

Site through the center of the compass and through the 200° marking of the compass housing. Pick out some landmark in the distance in the direction of your original destination. Walk to this landmark. At this point, take the same bearing toward another landmark until you reach your destination.

This method of finding your way to a specific destination using a compass and sighting from landmark to landmark can be used if you have only a rough map of the area but know the approximate area of your destination.

Assume you are in camp at "A" and one of your companions has met with an accident. A passing hunter informs you that there is a ranch house approximately four miles in a northwesterly direction from your camp and that there is a phone at this point. He draws you a map with the house and some landmarks he remembers on the route.

The victim is too badly injured to move over the rough terrain so you head out with the roughly drawn map, planning to phone for help and ask for a helicopter that can land near your camp.

Your sketch says that your first landmark is a tree, due north (azimuth 0°). You sight your compass at 0° and locate the tree and move to it, a distance of 800 steps from your starting point. The next landmark is a bare tree trunk at azimuth 30°, which you find with your sighting compass. In the same manner you proceed successively to each landmark shown on the sketch (next a large rock, then another tree with a blaze on it, then a rock slide, another pine tree), and you finally reach the ranch house in a little less than an hour and a half.

You might request that the helicopter pick you up at the ranch. Otherwise you will have to return via the same route you came, due to the obstacles. You, of

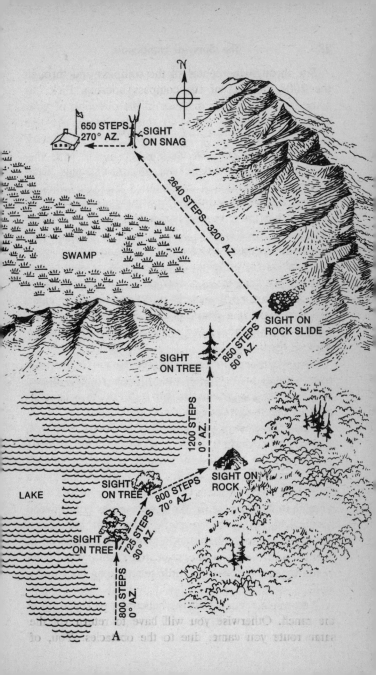

650 STEPS
270° AZ.

SIGHT
ON SNAG

2640 STEPS - 320° AZ.

SWAMP

850 STEPS
50° AZ.

SIGHT ON
ROCK SLIDE

SIGHT
ON TREE

1200
STEPS
0° AZ.

SIGHT ON
ROCK

SIGHT
ON TREE

800 STEPS
70° AZ.

LAKE

725 STEPS
30° AZ.

SIGHT
ON TREE

800 STEPS
0° AZ.

A

course, have given full details as outlined in the Mountain Rescue section later in these pages.

Returning to Your Original Destination

On your trip out you held the compass with the arrow pointing away from you, toward the place you were going to. Now that you want to retrace your steps back to your base camp, you do not have to reset the compass. Merely hold it so that the arrowpoint is facing you, instead of away from you, as it was when you came out. Orient the compass by turning your body until the north end of the compass needle points to the N of the compass housing. Locate a landmark in front of you that you can walk toward and use as a guide. At this landmark orient the compass again and pick another landmark as a guide, continuing this process until you have returned to your original base.

By using this simple method you don't have to reset your compass or remember complicated degree readings to follow. This method is useful if the weather is clear and you can find landmarks to walk toward.

However, you should know about back-sighting a course.

Backsighting, or Reverse Azimuth

When sighting at a back checkpoint, or if you wish to return the same way you came, you must remember to get an azimuth reading, which requires 180-degree plus or minus correction before it will be useful.

For instance, if your bearing or course of travel was on an azimuth reading of less than 180° (90°, or due east, for example), the correct back or reverse azimuth should read 270° (90° + 180°, or due west). If your original course or heading was on an azimuth of more than 180°, you must subtract 180° from the course run to fix the correct backsight. For example, the reverse azimuth of 280° would be 100° (280° − 180° = 100 degrees). By taking a back, or reverse, azimuth you can ascertain if you are on course.

How Far Is It?

You can determine how far you are traveling either by counting each time you take a double step, which is about five feet, or by estimating distance by the time it took you travel it.

For instance, it takes you about fifteen minutes to walk a mile on an open highway, twenty-five minutes to walk an open field, thirty minutes to walk through open woods and forty minutes to walk through forest or mountain foothills.

You can run a mile on an open highway in ten minutes, through an open field in thirteen minutes, through open woods in sixteen minutes and through forest in twenty-two minutes.

Which Type of Compass?

The cheaper coat lapel or pin-on sleeve models sold by some companies are difficult to hold still enough to get an accurate reading, and most have only four to eight cardinal points, include no sighting line and are not adjustable for declination. This type is only good for general direction finding, or to back up your regular compass in case it becomes inoperative.

A trail, roadhead, river or lake must be found exactly at the end of the compass course plotted. Otherwise, it might be missed by a few hundred yards if the woods are thick or visibility is poor.

It pays to purchase one of the better medium-priced compasses. Experienced woodsmen, mountaineers and explorers use a compass with a full 360-degree azimuth that has a sighting line and is adjustable for declination. They know that their life may be at stake if they make a forced landing, become lost or must find their way through wild, trackless country.

A medium-priced compass will range from $6.50 to $15.00. Silva, Inc., La Porte, Ind. 46350, manufactures several good models from $2.95 up. An excellent model is the Huntsman priced at $5.95. This compass dial is set off in 5-degree intervals, and can be used where the job isn't too exacting. Their Ranger model will of course do a better job and sells for $15.00.

Rangers use four types of compasses in fire-control work: the Forest Service Box Compass, the Silva Voyager, and the Leupold Sportsman and Cruiser models. These compasses range from $6.40 to $15.00 in price. The Sportsman and Cruiser models may be obtained from Leupold and Stevens Instruments, Inc., 4445 N.E. Glisan Street, Portland, Oregon 97213. All the compasses mentioned may be purchased at leading hardware, sporting goods and department stores.

Whichever model you buy, learn how to use it confidently, take good care of it, carry it with you whenever you are outdoors—and it may just save your life.

3

Orienting Yourself

Each year thousands of campers, hunters, fishermen and other recreationists stray off the marked forest trails and remote tote-roads, become confused or turned around—in other words, just plain lost! You would be surprised at the large number of adults who get mixed up. Many are experienced outdoorsmen who have become too complacent or careless.

Large sums of money are spent on search and rescue missions to find these unfortunate recreationists. It has been so costly, especially in the employment of aircraft used to search the vast areas of the Canadian Shield and Northwoods canoe areas, that restrictions have been placed on private recreational travel north of the 51st parallel.

With a larger recreation-minded population in the United States, the problem has jumped astoundingly. The rescue toll is so huge and expensive that some counties and rescue organizations have not been able to meet the financial drain. In many cases the rescued persons have been required to pay for the air and ground search in their behalf.

It is not uncommon to have several search and rescue missions going on at the same time in the Sierra Nevada

Range in California. In Washington, in one 24-hour period, I had to sit at my desk at the Lake Crescent headquarters and direct three search crews via radio. One crew was recovering the body of a victim who had slipped and fallen into a crevasse on the Blue Glacier, another crew was searching for a lost fisherman and the third crew was searching for a lost child near Eagle Lake.

At 11 P.M. I received word of a lost Boy Scout at the Sol Duc River Shelter. Since all my Rangers and fire-control aides were out on other missions, my wife took over communications, and I left with several friends and neighbors, and finally found the lad just at the approach of daylight. He had gone for water to a nearby stream, but in the dark he got turned around in the brush and dropped over a sheer 50-foot cliff at the edge of the Sol Duc River. He managed to land on both feet, but the shock of landing from such a height broke both his legs and an arm.

Route Finding

The material in this chapter differs from most information on the subject of how to find one's way after becoming lost. It employs a direct, step-by-step, non-technical approach, making it easier for a survivor or a lost person to decide on the direction that will take him to the nearest habitation. Using the methods outlined, he can reorient himself, even without a compass.

Man Cannot Walk a Straight Line

Basically, it is recognized that man cannot walk in a straight line without relying on some tangible clue.

Even if he could, rough terrain would usually prevent this. The clue may be a distant object such as an odd-shaped tree or peak that he can head directly to if the terrain will permit, or the clue may be the sound of rapids of a stream or a roaring waterfall that he can hear, giving him a direction by sound. Train and factory whistles or traffic sounds carry for long distances. A person can head in that direction.

Without a directional sound to guide him, man will gradually walk in a circle, so it is much safer to use a compass for route finding. When using a compass, we leave behind educated guesses as to direction and enter the area of scientific certainty.

Why We Become Lost

Generally, we get lost because we fail to relate our position to some known factor, natural or otherwise, as a directional guide, and or because of the lack of observation and systematic travel away from or return to a predetermined baseline (such as a trail, road, stream, powerline, river or lake shore, etc.). Going ahead with *only* a specific point in mind (such as a camp, hunting lodge, cabin, boat, car, etc.) is generally a mistake. These are a few of the reasons why we become confused and turned around.

Parking Your Vehicle

When a camper leaves his car on an old logging, fire or primitive tote-road and hikes, in a northwesterly direction, he does not merely head back in a general southeasterly direction to arrive at the point where he left his vehicle. (His compass, of course will help him do that.)

But there is more to a return route through the woods than that! In returning over rough or heavily timbered terrain the outdoorsman is apt to meander in a more or less zig-zag direction to avoid obstacles in the woods.

If he has gone any appreciable distance into the wilderness area, the chances are that he will find his car "missing" when he reaches the road that is his baseline, unless he has been very observant and picked out an easily recognized point near his parked car. The car is where he left it, but if he hasn't planned a logical return, he can get into trouble.

Using an Anchor Point

Unless he has an anchor point to direct him on reaching the road, he may come out of the woods a considerable distance to the right or left of his car, with bends in the road concealing the car from view. The confusing question he asks himself is: which direction shall I hike? Right or left?

Most logging and old tote-roads have many side roads and "Y" branches, unsigned, and with little or no current travel. If the camper reaches the road (his baseline), but is confused about whether to turn right or left, he will have to make a choice. If he doesn't spot his car after he has gone a mile or so in one direction, he should hike back in the opposite direction, where he will probably will run into his "lost" car.

Again, he may have arrived at a road which branched off from his base road. If this is the case, he will not find his car to the right or the left. If he is not an experienced woodsman, he may panic and get into a real jam.

Keeping Oriented

To avoid these confusing situations you must stay oriented by observing the terrain at all times. Before leaving your camp, car, canoe, boat or aircraft, look all around you and size up the country as far as you can see. Observe all the prominent landmarks such as peaks and bluffs to the right and left of you.

Make a mental note of what outstanding objects are back of your camp so that if you overrun your camp, you will know it. When you leave a road, trail, stream, river or ridge, note the side from which you left. Keep these as baselines.

Note the direction of the sun and prevailing breeze.

Keep track of how many streams you have crossed and recrossed, and how many ridges and passes you have traveled over.

Look back over your trail; it will look entirely different to you on returning!

These points cannot be overemphasized.

If you are heading out for a day's hike, and want to return before dark, travel until noon, eat your lunch, rest and then head back. Remember, head out half a day; return in the other half.

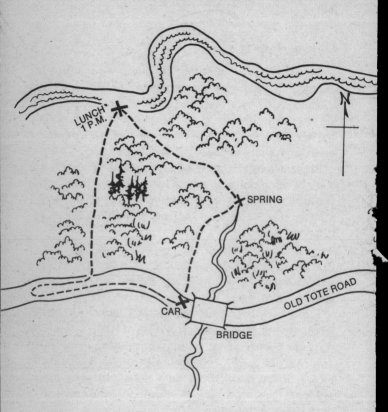

FINDING MISPLACED VEHICLE. *Hunter came in from the east on old tote road. He left his car at bridge. Left road at 6 A.M. Came to end of trail at spring. He then took off in a northwest direction. Had lunch at river. He left at 1 P.M. and decided to take a short cut and headed directly south, arriving on fire motorway at 5 P.M. He was confused, not knowing if his car was east or west of where he came out on the road. So he decided to turn right for half a mile. Not spotting his vehicle, he backtracked a mile and a half and saw his car at the bridge.*

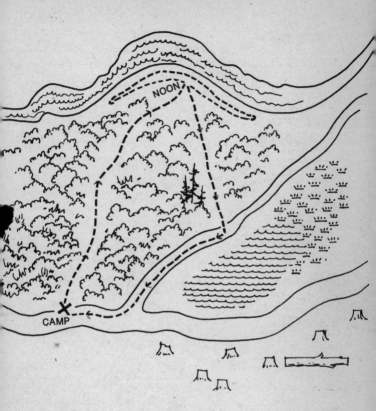

A fisherman came in over the old tote road on his trail bike from the east. He made an 8 A.M. camp near the junction of the fire lane and old tote road. He left his bike at camp since no motorized vehicles were allowed north of the fire road. He fished up and down stream, had lunch, and left at 2 P.M. He also decided to shortcut to his camp. However, due to the rough terrain he came out above his camp. He recognized where he was since he had observed the swamp, pond, and logged-over area across from the tote road. He then knew all he had to do was head down the tote road and keep to the right of the fire lane to reach his camp.

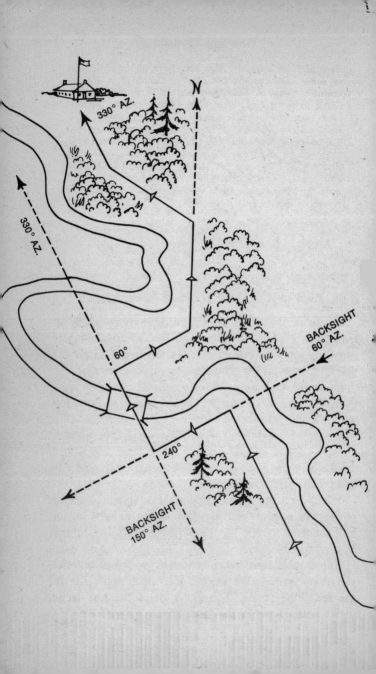

330° AZ.

N

330° AZ.

60°

BACKSIGHT
60° AZ.

240°

BACKSIGHT
150° AZ.

*Examples on opposite page and next on how a hiker
or other outdoorsman can clear obstacles if he has an
azimuth compass. Backsights are taken occasionally to
check to see if he is on course. If the compass sighting
course heading out is less than 180 degrees, to get backsight, add 180 degrees. If the forward course is more than
180 degrees, subtract 180 degrees to get backsight.
EXAMPLE A. The hiker starts out with a compass course
of 330°. He subtracts 180° to get his backsight. 330° −
180° = 150° backsight. Thus if he had to return back
over the same course from the Ranger Station, he would
return on his backsight courses.*

Basic Facts to Remember If You Become Lost

If you find yourself in unfamiliar country while attempting to return to your camp and are mixed up as
to which way to go, don't call yourself lost. At least not
yet! You may just be confused for a few minutes.

Don't panic. Thousands of people become lost each
year, but find their way out or are found by searchers
within a few hours or days.

Do this! Sit down and relax. Take some deep breaths.
Clear a spot of all inflammable forest litter and have a
smoke or chew some gum. Think things over, and stay
quietly for a few minutes.

When a person on foot first realizes he is not certain
of his whereabouts, he generally is not so far out that
he cannot be located, or, perhaps even relocate himself
in a reasonable time.

The trouble starts when a lost person keeps blunder-
ing along through the woods, increasing confusion for
the searching teams. Too many times the lost victim
walks entirely out of the search area.

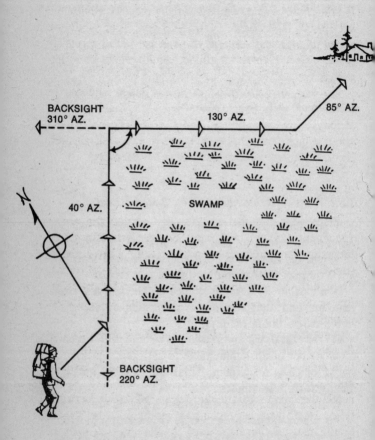

EXAMPLE B. *First leg of hunter's course is 85 degrees. If he wanted to know what his return or back sight is, he would add 180 degrees. 85° + 180° = 265°, the backsight.*

Get out Your Map and Compass

Find out which way is north and orient your map. If you don't have a compass, orient your map with the lay of the land. After comparing your map with the surrounding terrain, see if you can recognize some familiar object such as an alpine meadow, lake or a distant peak that you passed a short time back.

Go over in your mind the route taken and try to reconstruct your course since you left a known point. It may be closer than you think. If this doesn't work, climb a high point or tall tree and take a look around. Some distant object may refresh your memory.

Orienting with a Compass

Place your compass on the map next to the arrow (declination point) at the bottom right hand margin of the map that indicates magnetic north. This point is sometimes near the upper right-hand part of maps. Then turn the map until the compass needle points in the same direction as the arrow. Your map is now oriented. It's as simple as that!

Another way is to place the compass on the map so that its North and South coincide exactly with the vertical lines on the map. Turn the map and compass until north is at the top. Next, rotate the map underneath the compass until the degree difference between $0°$ or North and $180°$ compass marks and the North-South lines on the map equal the compass declination (variation) for that particular region. For example, if the declination is westerly, turn the map toward the right to correct for the number of degrees of compass declination shown on your map; if the declination is easterly, turn the map the other way, to the left. Now your map is oriented to true north.

How to Use Barriers

If your map shows that you are east or west of a river road, trail or power line that indicates that these barriers run in a generally northerly direction, you can head due east or west as the case may be and arrive at one of these landmarks in a day or so and find your way out from there.

Railroad, power and phone line right-of-ways are patrolled fairly regularly, and someone will be along soon to help you on your way.

Don't forget the sun can give you a rough east or west direction, depending on the time of day.

In some instances you will not have a map or compass. Under these conditions a general direction is not always good enough, nor are "nature's signposts," such as moss that is supposed to grow on the north side of trees. Therefore, you must resort to an "in-the-field" method that is both quick, simple and accurate.

Unless you are aware of the limitations of the "Old Eskimo Watch," Equal Shadow, Shortest Shadow and Hour Methods found in most outdoor and old military manuals, you really can get into a mess. All these systems have sound astronomical principles, but each has its limitations and might further confuse you.

The New Owendoff Method

Illustrated in the box is the latest and most accurate method of finding time and direction quickly without a compass. It is called the Owendoff Shadow-tip method of Determining Time and Direction. It was worked out and copyrighted by Robert S. Owendoff of Falls Church, Virginia, when he was 16. Mr. Owendoff is now an officer in the United States Navy.

Government agencies and various military departments have edited their manuals to take account of this timesaving method. Some encyclopedias are being revised to include this new method in their new issues.

Orienting Without a Compass

Orient your map by rotating it until the direction of a line drawn from any point to any other point on the map will be true direction between the two points on the ground.

Another method requires that the observer's position on the map be known as nearly as possible, and that one point shown on the map—such as a high peak— can be identified on the land.

An imaginary line must be drawn between the observer's position on the map and the position of the identified point. The map is then turned around until the line, if extended, passes through the point on the land. The map is then oriented, and the lines drawn from the position occupied to the other point on the map will pass through actual points on the terrain.

If you do not know your approximate location on the map, but notice two peaks in line on the ground in a distance, spread the map out on as flat a surface as you can find and locate them on your map. Line the two peaks up on the map and turn the map until, when sighting across the two peaks on the map, they are in line with the two peaks on the ground. You are somewhere along this line of sight.

By using the map scale, you can measure the distance between the two points.

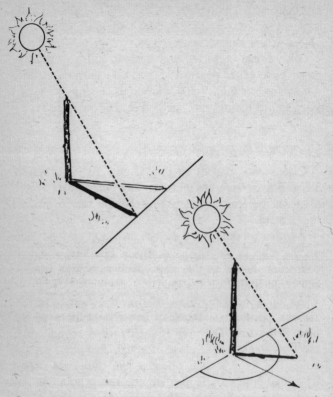

Finding Direction by Locating the North Star. SHADOW-
TIP METHOD. *To find direction, mark the tip of the
shadow cast from a 3-foot stick, which may be inclined
to obtain a more convenient shadow length. Mark tip
again after ten minutes. A straight line through the two
marks is an east-west line, from which any desired direction of travel can be found by adding the other compass points to the line. To find the time of day, proceed
as for direction, then draw a noon line at right angles to
east-west line at any point. Move stick to where these
lines intersect, and set it vertically. The shadow is now
an hour hand on your 24-hour "shadow clock." 6 A.M.
is west and 6 P.M. is east. In the above example, the time
is 9:30 A.M.*

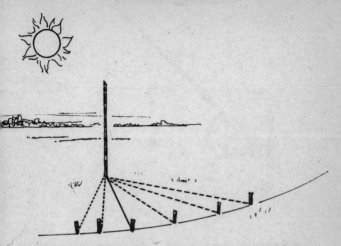

SHORTEST SHADOW METHOD. *Put up a stick or rod as nearly vertical as possible in a level place. Check the alignment of the stick by sighting along the line of a makeshift plum bob. Before midday, begin marking the position of the end of the stick's shadow. Continue marking until the shadow definitely lengthens. The time of the shortest shadow is when the sun passes the local meridian, which was the solar noon.*

If you can line up another peak or butte, lookout tower or other point at an angle opposite the above sighting, you will have an exact "fix," and you will know your position both on the map and the ground.

Finding Your Way Without Map or Compass

The experts say you can't get lost if you have a compass and map. If nothing else, you can back-sight by back-reading your compass or you can walk to a land-

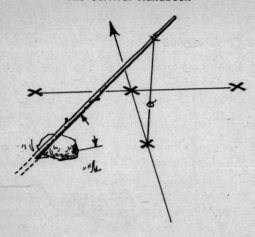

HOUR METHOD. *Hang a rock from the end of a stick propped at a 45 degree angle to the ground. At some time before noon, mark the spot where the rock's shadow falls. Approximately six hours later, mark the spot where the afternoon sun casts the rock's shadow. Draw a line from the point directly under the suspended rock through a point halfway between the morning and afternoon mark. This line points to within 3 degrees of true north.*

mark you can see and set a new course on your map from that new position. However, if you have lost your map and compass and cannot find your way back to your base, there are still other ways you can find yourself.

Three common ways to relocate yourself are by re-circling the area, going over it in small squares, or cruising it. Here is how these methods work.

The Circle Method

- Picture a wagon wheel with the spokes pointing in all directions.
- Blaze a tree on all four sides with your knife, ax or the edge of a sharp rock to use as a hub or anchor point.
- Next, walk in a more or less straight line to search for your tracks. Walk as far as you can without losing sight of your anchor tree. Mark another tree in line with your original anchor tree. Blaze it on both sides so that you can find your way back to camp if necessary. Keep repeating this method of search, returning to your anchor point, walking in an opposite direction, blazing a tree, returning, until you have completely circled the area.
- If you are not successful in finding your trail, keep heading out until you find your old footprints. They have to be somewhere along the edge of the search circle. You may have to extend each search heading for half a mile or so before you cut your original tracks.
- If you cannot trace your way out, the best plan is to stay at your camp until found. If you finally decide you must walk out, leave a note fastened to your anchor tree with your name, physical condition, direction of travel and the time you left camp.
- Mark your path as you go along with blazes on trees, rock cairns or arrows made with stones pointing your direction every few hundred yards to help searchers track you.

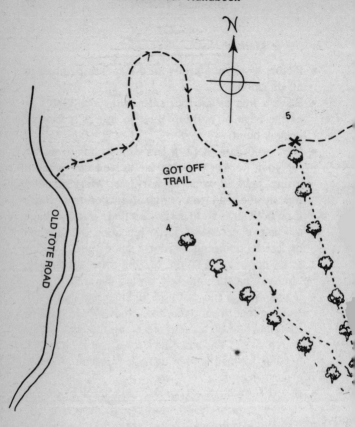

THE CIRCLE METHOD OF FINDING YOUR WAY OUT. *A hiker decided to backpack into Bear Lake to fish. Since this section of forest was closed to trail bikes, he left his machine hidden just off an old tote road and headed up the trail, which meandered in a northeasterly direction. While enjoying the scenery, and not being very observant, he missed the trail in a bend. He knew at this time that he was heading in a southerly direction, but thought that he would cut the main trail where it might loop somewhere. However, darkness overtook him, so he made an emergency bivouac camp at a spring. In the*

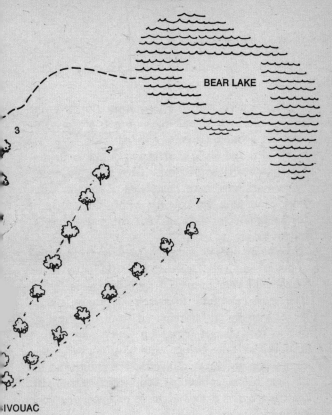

morning a dense fog moved in, and he was unable to
determine the general direction of the sun. So he decided to try the circle method he had heard about used
by Boy Scouts and Rangers. Sighting a nearby tree, he
blazed it on four sides to use as an anchor tree. So that
he could travel in a more or less straight line, he lined
trees ahead of him and blazed each one with an out-
going blaze and one on the back side so that he could
return to his camp if necessary. He walked for approximately half a mile on several legs of the spoke,
and on the fifth try he found the Bear Creek trail.

The Square Method

The pattern suggested is to walk a series of concentric squares.

- Walk in a particular direction in as straight a line as you can for a given length of time or for a distance of a one-quarter to one-half mile.
- Next, turn and walk at right angles the same distance as nearly as you can. Turn right again and again until you have completed a square, carefully examining the country within and adjacent to the square for sight of your camp or some familiar terrain.
- If the camp doesn't come into view on the first try, a larger and still larger square will have to be hiked until your misplaced camp or car is found.
- You must be careful that each succeeding square is not visually so far removed from the previous one as to endanger bypassing your camp.
- If darkness falls before you have located your camp, stop and make a bivouac camp and wait till daylight before continuing your search. Don't risk the chance of a woods accident or bypassing your camp in the dark.

The Cruising Method

You think you are in the general vicinity of your camp, but the forest cover is so dense you cannot see for any appreciable distance. You don't know whether camp is to your right or left; perhaps it is just a short distance ahead of you, or again you may have passed it a short distance back. In a situation like this you can

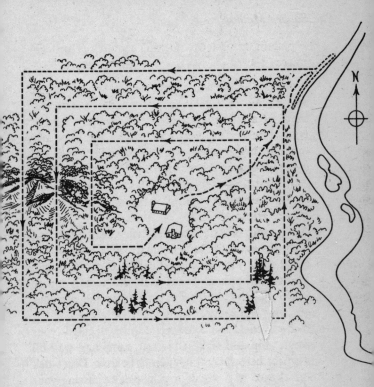

THE SQUARE METHOD. *A
camper bivouacked at an isolated spring decides to fish
the Swan River, which he knows lies due east of his
wilderness camp. He leaves at 5 A.M. and travels in a
northeasterly direction through heavy brush and timber.
He reaches the river at 10 A.M. and fishes up- and downstream. Has lunch at noon and leaves at 2 P.M. The forest
litter prevents him from back tracking the way he came
to river—so decides to use the square method in reaching
his camp. Knows that his camp lies somewhere west of
the river, but isn't sure just where. He heads due west.
On his third square he finally sights his camp.*

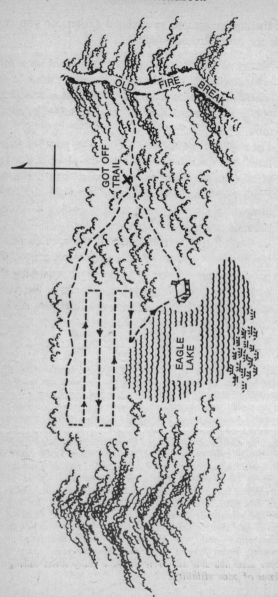

4

Signaling

Your survival depends upon four things: shelter from the elements, food, water and signaling to searchers so that you can be rescued.

A man lost in endless back country—even a downed aircraft in the woods—is not easy to see from the air. Sometimes weeks pass before air-rescue units locate downed planes in areas like the Sierra-Nevada range.

So your signals are extremely important if you are to be found. They must make you a larger target, a person distinct from your environment, and thus easier to locate.

Begin almost at once to plan your signals. Select the location for them carefully and gather together the materials you will need so that you can put them to use as soon as you hear a plane's engine. Too often campers are missed because they cannot start their fires or use their signal mirrors until the rescue plane has passed them.

Don't use your signals indiscriminately. You may need them to guide later rescue efforts, or to attract searching planes that missed you the first or second or third trip out.

It is not easy to spot signals from the air. The three smoke signals in the center of the field (centerground) were made by campers whose stalled jeeps can be seen on the road at the right. Remember to make your signals as large as you can.

Naturally, the type of signal you use will depend on the material you have available and the particular situation you are in.

Fires

The best signal is fire—a huge bright one at night, a smoky one by day. Maintain a good supply of fuel to give the appropriate signal. Build your signal fire on the highest point near your shade or shelter.

If fuel is plentiful, three fires some distance apart are better than one. (Three of anything is universally recognized as a distress signal.)

Here again your object is to create a signal that will contrast with your background. Against snow, dark smoke is most effective. Against dark green woods, white smoke is more easily seen.

Try to create a distinct column of smoke that will rise high over the treetops and contrast with the sky. If the skies are overcast, use dark smoke; against clear skies, light smoke.

To make black smoke put engine oil, rags soaked in oil, pieces of rubber or matting into your fire. To make white smoke put green leaves, moss, ferns or a little water into the fire.

You will have to prepare your fire ahead of time, lighting it only when you hear a rescue plane. Or you might maintain a small fire and add fuel to it when you hear a plane.

Fortunately for lost campers, most wilderness areas in summer and fall are under constant surveillance for fire by forest spotters. As soon as you start your fire, if it is large and smoky, it will be seen by rangers and investigated.

In the late fall and winter months it is best to build three fires in a triangle shape about fifty feet apart. Generally, lookout towers will not be manned after the heavy fall rains set in. However, three fires indicates trouble. Search aircraft pilots and observers will know that you need help, and that you are not just a hunter trying to keep warm and waving at them while standing near a bonfire to keep warm!

Be careful that you do not start a forest fire. Your object is not to destroy the entire area, merely to be seen.

Signal Mirrors

A signal mirror is an excellent device for attracting attention, particularly of aircraft. Such mirrors can be obtained at Army-Navy or camping-equipment stores, and the directions are included. See the illustration. It is a two-faced metallic mirror with a hole in the center. You can improvise one from a can lid that is shiny on both sides.

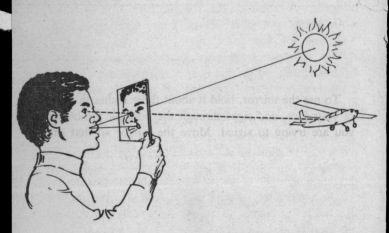

HOW TO USE SIGNALING MIRROR. *Hold the mirror a few inches from your face and sight at airplane through hole. Spot of light through hole will fall on face, hand, or shirt. Adjust angle of mirror until reflection of light spot in rear of mirror disappears through hole while you are sighting an airplane through hole. Do not continue to flash mirror in direction of plane after receipt of signal has been acknowledged.*

I	II	X	F	≫	K
1. Require doctor — serious injuries	2. Require medical supplies	3. Unable to proceed	4. Require food and water	5. Require firearms and ammunition	6. Indicate direction & proceed
↑	I⟩	⌐⌐	△	LL	L
7. Am preceeding in this direction	8. Will attempt to take off	9. Aircraft badly damaged	10. Probably safe to land here	11. All well	12. Require fuel and oil
N	Y	⫪	W	▢	!
13. No — negative	14. Yes — affirmative	15. Not understood	16. Require engineer	17. Require compass & map	18. Require signal lamp

Ground-air emergency code.

To use the mirror, hold it about three inches in front of your face, and sight through the hole on the object you are trying to signal. Move the mirror so that the light spot on your face, which you can see in reflection, disappears in the hole in the mirror while you are still maintaining sight of the plane through the hole.

On a clear day ground signals may be transmitted for ten miles, signals to attract an aircraft can be seen an even greater distance.

Signaling Materials

Anything you have with you which will make you distinct from the environment can be used for signaling. Bright colored clothing, aluminum foil, colored tarps,

A	1	H	8	O		V	
B	2	I	9	P		W	
C	3	J		Q		X	
D	4	K	0	R		Y	
E	5	L		S		Z	
F	6	M		T		NUMERALS TO FOLLOW	
G	7	N		U		LETTERS TO FOLLOW	(J)

Semaphore letters are made by holding two flags at different angles. The letters appear this way as you face the sender.

can all be used. If you have a white piece of material, climb a tall tree and improvise a flag with a pole lashed to the top.

Shadow Signals

If you have no material with you, you may have to make signals which will use the sun to cast shadows. For best effectiveness, make three such signals oriented to the sun.

In areas near the equator, a north-south line will give you a good shadow, except at noon. Areas farther north or south need an east-west line to make a good shadow.

Stamp or dig out S O S characters and pile dirt or rocks or foliage along one side of the characters to make the shadows more distinct. In snow country, snow can be piled along one side of the characters to emphasize the characters. Be sure to make the letters large enough to be seen from a plane.

Sound

Signals made by sound are the least effective. As with visual signals, three of whatever sound you can make denotes "Distress." A "thunder" type whistle is recom-

Trail markers are important signals, too. The stones at top indicate a left turn; the broken branch at top indicates a right turn. The broken sapling is turned in the direction of travel. At bottom are stone markers indicating straight ahead and right turn.

mended as an easy way to make a lot of noise. Blowing across the mouth of an empty large-caliber cartridge case makes a distinctive sound. If you have a gun, shoot once, wait ten seconds and fire twice more about five seconds apart. The first will attract attention and the second and third will give direction. If there is no answer, save your ammunition. Sound carries best during the early evening quiet just before dark.

If you can cut a circular path that is 12 feet wide and 75 feet in diameter, it could be an effective signal for it disturbs the natural pattern of the terrain. A trampled field of grass or a medium-sized burned-out area can also be spotted easily.

Remember. Have your signals ready for use on short notice. Do not use them so that you put yourself in danger.

5

Shelters

If you do any wilderness traveling, you'll find there are many situations where you will need a sudden emergency shelter.

Perhaps a thunder and lightning storm has halted you, or an out-of-season snowstorm looks as if it is gathering on the mountaintops. Again, a member of your party has been seriously injured, or perhaps your pack animals became frightened and deserted you.

Whatever your reason, you suddenly need to do what the animals do, that is, burrow in and protect yourself against the elements.

The type of shelter you make depends on whether you need protection from rain, wind, cold, heat or insects. It also depends on whether the shelter is to be used only for a one night stand or for a possibly indefinite period. For an overnight stay in a forested area it is more efficient to burrow or hollow out a small shelter under a downed tree than to construct a shelter. If this is not practical and you determine that you need a shelter, there is natural material in the woods and mountains that can be used for a windbreak or a lean-to shelter.

Here are some outdoor shelters that can be built in various ways. Top left, *the lean-to is a semi-permanent home that can be fashioned out of cloth, as shown, or twigs, branches, and boughs. Face it to side of prevailing wind. Top right is a smaller, less complex version. Center is a shelter dug into high snow. Bottom left is a simple tent that can be useful if you have the rope and tarp and if you want to break camp each morning. Bottom right shows what can be done with available materials, like the canoe.*

*If you have a parachute or similar cloth, you can build
a tepee or a simple shelter that will last for quite a while.
If your plane has crashed, you can use it as a base for
your wilderness home.*

A Few Pointers

Here are a few general rules to follow:

- Pick your campsite carefully. First, reconnoiter
  the area and see if there is an abandoned cabin,
  ranch house or miner's shack nearby. You might

even find a snow surveyor's cabin. Most of these are well stocked with food, sleeping bags and equipment for winter patrols. Finding a ready-made shelter will save time and energy.

- Don't build a shelter at the base of a steep slope or cliff or in any area where you might run the risk of a rock or snow avalanche. Don't build under dead trees or snags that might fall on you or your shelter. Build in a sheltered place protected from high winds when possible.

- If you can do so safely, camp in thick woods so that you can be near fuel and out of the wind. The ideal spot is near both fuel and water.

- Keep the front openings of shelters cross-wind. This will prevent sparks from setting your woods home or aircraft on fire. A windbreak made from small down logs, snow or ice blocks set close together to block the wind will make your forced stay more comfortable.

- Use any safe natural barrier, rock or log windbreak for a shelter.

- Don't build your emergency camp in a stream bed or canyon, where a flash flood miles away may come crashing down in the night, washing your camp or shelter away under tons of water and debris. Flash floods sometimes crest from six to twenty feet deep!

Open-sided Shelter

In wilderness areas where there are boughs and limbs available an open-sided shelter is easy to build and will provide some protection from rain, wind or snow.

Mountain rescue personnel advocate the simple, under-the-log shelter made by piling logs or boughs

Indian Tepee. Students at the USAF Survival School in Fairchild, Washington, learn to build an Indian tepee from their parachutes. The tepee is the best all-around shelter for it permits building a fire inside it.

A-Frame. This A-frame shelter is made from a tarp or parachute hitched to logs. The bed is made of pine boughs.

against a fallen tree. To build one, find a tree that has some space underneath it. Pile up whatever logs or tree branches you can find. Plug the holes with slabs of bark. Keep your living area small and snug.

Or bend a limber sapling over, tie a rope on the upper end and stake the other end down to the ground at the desired height. Next, trim off the top and inside branches and use them to cover the sides. Cut more green branches as needed to make the shelter more wind- and snowproof. Adding a ground cloth or tarpaulin will help make it more waterproof.

Tepee Shelter

One of the best shelters for snow or drizzly weather and to keep insects out is the Indian tepee made on a smaller scale with a cloth, poncho, canvas tarpaulin or parachute. In this shelter you can cook, eat, sleep, dress and make smoke, all without stepping outside. If you should fall asleep, your warming fire smoke will weave out through the top as an emergency signal.

Lean-to

You can make a simple lean-to shelter from nearby brush or by placing a rope or pole between two trees or stakes and draping a bivouac cloth, tarpaulin or parachute over it; make the corners and sides fast with stones or pegs. When constructing any type of shelter, take the time to do a good job. Your comfort will depend on it. The frame can be made from wind-thrown dead pole trees or you can cut some green ones as needed. Cover the frame with whatever you have or with green leafy branches.

Aircraft Shelter. If you crash land your plane, you

can drape a parachute, blanket or whatever cloth you
have over one wing. Make the corners and sides secure
with rocks or dirt piled along the edges to anchor the
material. Both the aircraft and shelter must be well
anchored, or a sudden squall could play havoc with
your primitive home.

A rubber life raft, boat or canoe turned over or
tipped up against a log or rock will give some shelter

*Lean-to Tent. This is another version of the lean-to
shelter made from boughs. This one is covered with a
tarp. A fire can be made in front of the tent.*

from the elements. More protection will be gained if a tarpaulin or canvas sheet is draped over the middle or at one end of a canoe or other object.

Bivouac Sheet

A bivouac sheet, poncho or ground cloth can serve many useful purposes. It can be used for a ground sheet and add insulation. It can act as a roof for a snow house or a cave. A lean-to can be made with it. When mountain climbing if caught without any type of shelter during a severe wind, rain or snowstorm, it can save your life.

Hole-in-the Snow

This is another type of tree shelter. If the snow is four or more feet deep, you can build the snow hole. Find a tree that has limbs down to snow or ground level. Dig out all the snow around the tree trunk down to the ground and out to the desired diameter. You can use a ski, snowshoe or a cooking pot for a snow shovel. Trim all branches inside the hole and use them to thatch over the rooftop. Cut more bushy branches nearby to line the bottom and to finish the top. Your fire must be built on top of green limbs or small green logs to keep it from becoming wet-out. A small ditch should be dug on the low side of the shelter for melting snow to drain into. This type of shelter is difficult for search aircraft to spot from the air unless a good cloud of smoke rises from it.

The Snow Trench

The snow trench is easy to make. Dig down to the desired depth (usually four or five feet), line the bot-

Bedroll from Blankets. 1. Spread blankets, one on top of the other. 2. Fold top blanket to within six inches of opposite corner. 3. Fold over flap to close edge opening. 4. Shift top blanket to within six inches of other edge of lower blanket. 5. Fold lower blanket over top blanket. 6. Fold over flap to close edge opening of bottom blanket. 7. Turn bottom up one or twice. Use two blanket pins to hold bottom edge, two to hold each side.

tom with pine or other evergreen boughs. You can use tree poles, skis or snowshoes for roof beams and cover with boughs or a tarpaulin. All snow shelters should be provided with a ditch at one end for melting snow to drain into.

Igloos and Snow-Block Houses

These are generally too difficult and time-consuming to build. The snow has to be of the proper consistency and well packed before it can be cut or shaped into snow or ice blocks. Emergency shelters should be easy and quick to construct since they are short-time shelters.

Blanket Shelters

There are two excellent sporting "space" blankets on the market that are a boon to campers. Personally, I believe that every person entering a wilderness area should pack one with his equipment. I do, myself, for safety, and believe me it has saved me several times from cold-weather illness when I needed its protection during a sudden blizzard.

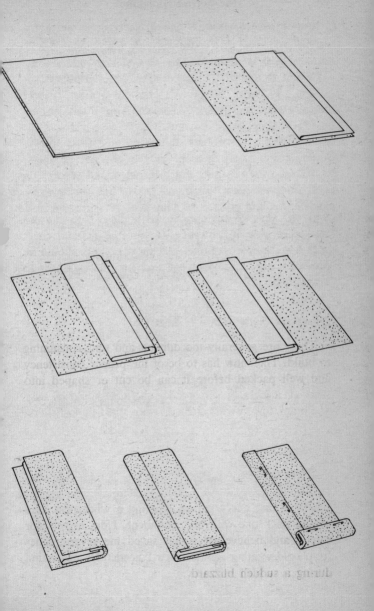

Both blankets are 84 x 56 inches in size, but their weight and cost are considerably apart. The NRC blanket lists at under $3.00—less at discount stores.

National Research Corporation, a subsidiary of Norton, 37 East Street, Winchester, Mass. 01890, manufactures the Rescue Blanket. This little gem is based on superinsulation and was proved effective in space missions. It weighs only two ounces. It works by reflecting ninety percent of the covered person's body heat while keeping out rain, wind and snow.

Another excellent "thermos" product is the Sportsman's blanket, a product of King-Seeley-Thermos Company, Norwich, Conn. 06856. It is priced under $10, and is a heavier blanket than the one above, weighing twelve ounces. It is ideal for most outdoor activities where a protecting cover is required. It is used by rangers and other outdoorsmen. I have used both blankets during several search and rescue missions in cold and wet weather. The blankets are very versatile. They not only keep you warm and dry, but can be used to catch water when it rains and to reflect campfire heat back into your emergency tent or shelter. They will reflect radar, which can be a help in some situations. They can be laid out as ground signals for searching aircraft, too.

The Tube Tent

This is another item that can be a helpful tool for the go-light backpacker and can be used for an emergency tent. It is light and rainproof. The heavy-gauge polyethylene, usually nine feet in circumference and nine feet long, can be set up in moments as a tent by quickly running a nylon rope through the tube and tying each end to a sturdy tree.

Your body and pack keeps the floor anchored down flat. Sometimes when the wind is strong, I have added two rocks just inside at each end of the opening to help stabilize the tent. Don't close the tent openings. It can be dangerous because the material is water- and air-proof.

Sometimes if the weather is inclement, I use three Visklamps: one in the center on top of the tube and one at each end, with the top one pulling the center a few inches high at the ridge, and the two end ones pulling down about one foot. This helps to keep out sleet and rain. Otherwise the rope ridge usually sags in the middle. Visklamps weigh only a few ounces. They are attached by pulling several inches of the material into the loop (the metal loops are shaped like a dumb-bell). Next, a small rubber ball is inserted into the loop of wire. This holds the tube material and will not tear it. The other end is fastened to an overhanging limb, if there is one or some improvised device directly over the center. The other clamps are fastened so that a cord or line pulls the ends of the top of the tube downward about one foot.

6

Fires and Cooking

Fire has been man's friend since the beginning of time; it also has been his enemy when he has let it get out of control. Under emergency conditions, it can be one of your greatest comforts and assets. You will need a fire for warmth, keeping dry, cooking, signaling or for purifying questionable water. The following suggestions will inform you where it is safe to build a fire and how to build it with or without matches.

Preparing the Fire

Prepare the location of your fire *very carefully*. To be safe, build it on a sandbar, flat rock or other safe place, clear of all forest debris and litter.

- If possible, clear a circle ten feet in diameter down to mineral soil (damp bare soil), and build your fire in the center.
- If you have to build it in the woods, build it away from rotten logs and stumps, brush fields, dry grass, low overhanging trees or other inflammable materials. Clear away leaves, pine needles, moss, so that you do not start an uncontrollable fire. (If the fire does get away from you, you may

have to pay a very expensive fire control bill after you are rescued!)

- If the fire must be built on wet or muddy ground, in a swamp or on snow or ice, build a platform of flat rocks or green logs and make your fire on top. Be careful not to use rocks from a stream bed. There is moisture in these rocks and they may explode when heated. Use rocks or stones from farther up the bank.

- Never build your fire under low-hanging limbs. You may make a torch out of the tree and have an uncontrolled fire! Never build your fire under a snow-laden tree. The melting snow will drown it.

- Don't waste fire-making materials. Your very life may depend on being able to start a fire and keep it going.

- Don't waste your matches trying to light a poorly constructed fire. Don't waste matches for lighting your smokes—get a light from a coal or a lighted twig.

- Dry damp or wet wood near your campfire so you can use it later, but be watchful that a wind-blown spark doesn't set the woodpile afire.

- Save some of the driest tinder and wood for easy fire starting in the morning.

- To make a fire last overnight, place several large logs on it so the fire will burn into the center of the pile. After a good bed of coals has formed, cover them lightly with ashes and dry dirt. The fire should be smoldering in the morning.

- If your logs are too long, you can lay them star-shaped across the center of the fire. When the center has burned out, all you have to do is keep pushing the burned ends into the center. This is a handy method when you do not have an axe or saw.

- You can break long, sound dry limbs to proper length by breaking them over a sharp rock edge.
- Don't leave your fire unattended! A breeze may spring up and burn your bivouac camp, or start a forest fire that could overtake you and damage the surrounding country for miles.

Firewood

Twigs and small branches, materials that are often called "squaw wood," that are lying on the ground are usually damp or wet and are hard to ignite. However, any forest litter during the summer months in dry weather will ignite and burn rapidly.

Dried and fallen cones of the various conifers are generally pitchy. They make excellent tinder and will burn briskly and long enough to ignite your kindling. Knock the limbs from a rotten windfall log and usually you will find chunks of resinous wood at the butt of the limb. Pine knots from standing dead snags usually contain "pine-fat," or pitch. Sometimes you can dig pitchy wood out of old rotten stumps. You can even make green wood burn if you split it fine enough and if you have plenty of dry kindling to create sufficient heat.

In treeless regions there are some natural fuels: dry grass, which can be twisted into bunches; dead bushes; peat dry enough to burn (found at the top of undercut old river banks); dry animal dung and animal fats. And you can use motor fuels from your disabled vehicle.

To get the most warmth from your fire, build a reflector in back of your fire with foil, or use a reflector made from green logs or a slab of rock. Sometimes the fire can be placed against a large rock slab which will reflect the fire's heat toward you or your shelter.

How to Start a Fire Without Matches

There are a number of ways to start a fire without using matches or a cigarette lighter. None of them is easy!

Some writers of outdoor manuals say a fire can be started by using the lens from a camera, binoculars or eyeglasses, by using shotgun shells, or rifle cartridges— and there's always the old Boy Scout bow and drill method. They even say that a satisfactory lens can be made from thin ice by shaving and smoothing it with the warm hand so it is like a magnifying glass. No doubt at some time all but the latter have lighted fires under ideal conditions (I would like to know how the melting ice water was kept off the dry tinder—this wasn't mentioned in the manual). Nor do these writers tell how difficult it is to start a fire with the above methods in a wet forest or even under ideal conditions at home when using all dry tinder. It has been done, but it is almost impossible. However, these methods will be explained for what they are worth.

THE BURNING GLASS. Any convex lens two inches or more in diameter can be used in bright sunlight to concentrate the sun's rays on dry prepared tinder, and a fire will begin. If you have a small six-power magnifying glass in your "stampede kit," it will work to better advantage, and you can save your precious matches.

STARTING A FIRE WITH FIREARMS. Pry a bullet from a cartridge by loosening the bullet from the casing. Do this by laying it on a rock and tapping all around the neck of the casing with a stone or the back of your knife. The bullet can then be worked out with your fingers. If you are packing a shotgun, uncrimp the top of the shell and remove the wadding, all of the shot and most of the powder. Make the fire ready by having all the dry tinder at hand. Then stuff a small piece of dry, frayed cloth into the cartridge or shell hull. Fire the weapon up into the air. Quickly pick up the piece of glowing cloth. Blow it into a flame, place it on the tinder and nurse it along until the tinder ignites. This isn't always successful and is sometimes wasteful of ammunition.

FIRE STARTING. Top, *the bow-and-drill method and "burning glass" method.*

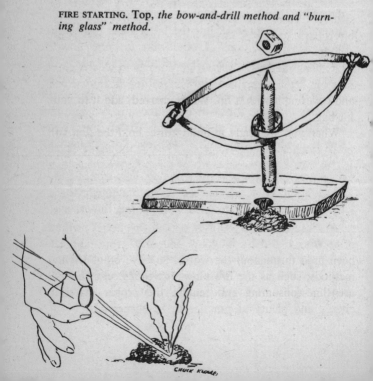

THE CUTTING TORCH METHOD. At many auto supply and hardware stores you can purchase for less than a dollar a small aluminum spark lighter that welders use to light their cutting torches. This little gadget is only six inches long and weighs two ounces. The gas lighter contains a small aluminum cup that directs the strong heavy sparks downward if directed onto any dry tinder when the handles are squeezed rapidly together.

THE OLD FLINT AND STEEL METHOD. This method was the fire starter for the early explorers and pioneers. With it they lighted not only their fires, but ignited their flintlock firearms. The kit was carried in a buckskin bag and contained punk tinder to catch sparks, flint or quartz-pyrite, a piece of steel and, of course, the prepared tinder. The tinder must be very dry to light by sparks. Tinder can consist of shredded cedar bark, birch bark, cotton or any other material that will ignite readily.

A quick method of preparing punk is to char a piece of cloth by lighting it and then putting it into a can and covering it with a lid. When charred, add it to your kit bag.

When you are ready to build a fire, hold the flint and punk catcher in your fingers, the wicking about $\frac{1}{8}$ to $\frac{1}{16}$ of an inch from the edge of the flint. Next, strike a glancing blow vertically with a piece of steel or the back of your knife blade. As the tinder ignites, gently blow it into a flame and place it on the kindling.

THE BOW AND DRILL METHOD. The Boy Scout method of starting a fire by the bow and drill procedure has been used throughout the world. So have other friction methods, such as the fire plow, fire-thong, etc., but all are time-consuming and require the proper material, energy and plenty of practice to be successful.

You will need a bow, with a thong long enough to loop around a small piece of limb and a spindle to serve as a drill against a fireboard. A hardwood top to hold the spindle is necessary, too. The top is held tightly down against the spindle. By moving the bow rapidly back and forth and rotating the drill in the fireboard, so much friction is generated that the residue collected at the bottom of the "V" in the board will start smoldering. Gently blow the debris into a flame and place on the dry tinder.

A QUICK, MODERN WAY. Carry a leakproof cigarette lighter in your survival pack. Add several extra wicks and flints in the top of the lighter and wrap tightly in waterproof tape. If you are careful and do not expose the flame for prolonged periods, you can get from 400 to 600 lights with it.

WATERPROOF MATCHES. Be careful when striking these; the heads break off easily. Save matches by using a candle. You will need only one match to light it. If you haven't a candle, make a prayer-stick (feather- or fuzz-stick, as it is called sometimes). It is made from seasoned softwood that has been whittled so that the shavings still attached to it bristle out in all directions. Several of these, eight to twelve inches long, piled criss-cross under dry kindling, will start the larger fuel burning.

SPECIAL FIRE MAKERS. The new Metal Match starts fires when you and your regular matches are soaking wet. With careful use, this modern match will make up to 3,000 lights. Every sportsman should have one in his pack.

FUSÉE METHOD. If you have a "fusée" signal flare in your aircraft, car or boat—the type used by police at scenes of accidents—you can light it to start a fire by scraping the cap end on a rock. Read and follow the directions, but be careful not to set the woods on fire.

THE FLINT-STICK consists simply of a flint imbedded in a tiny plastic handle. By scraping the flint with the sharp edge of a steel blade, you can produce a very high temperature spark that will ignite any type of dry tinder. These two metal matches are a modern version of the old pioneer's flint and steel. They really work.

ELECTRIC SPARK METHOD. If you have made a forced landing in your aircraft, or if your boat has been wrecked on an isolated beach and you do not have a radio transmitter on board, you can still build an SOS signal if your starter battery isn't too badly smashed. Get some dry tinder ready and direct the sparks on the

READY

Gather tinder (dry wood shavings, paper, grass, leaves, cloth, bark) and prepare camp fire material in usual manner.

AIM

Use sharp instrument (knife, sharp rock, glass) to *slowly* carve small particles down into concentrated area on tinder.

FIRE!

Scrape Metal Match *fast* . . . throwing sparks on concentrated particles and you have instant fire! It's that simple.

prepared tinder by shorting the negative and positive terminal wires together. If you do have a radio transmitter that is not damaged, get off an SOS May Day immediately. Give your location as accurately as you can. Before the battery becomes too weak, start a fire with the remainder of the juice. A search plane can spot you more readily when there is a tall column of smoke rising above brush and trees.

BURNING AIRCRAFT OR BOAT FUEL. You can improvise a stove to burn gasoline, outboard motor fuel, lubricating oil or a mixture of these. Put one or two inches of sand or fine gravel in the bottom of a can or other container and add gasoline or a mixture of gas an oil. Be careful when lighting—the fuel may flash! Stand back a safe distance and toss a lighted match or piece of paper into the can. After the first flash the flame will die down to a steady small fire.

Deciding the Type of Fire Needed

Your next step is to decide what type of fire you will need, and how to build it.

THE SIGNAL FIRE. Probably you will never need a signal fire. However, on several occasions over the years while directing search and rescue missions, I have found men who died because they failed to build one.

The purpose of a signal fire is to attract the attention of a fire lookout or forest patrolman, search aircraft or others who will rescue you. You will need such a fire when someone in camp is seriously ill or badly injured and cannot be left alone while you go for assistance. Or it may be you who is lost, sick or injured!

THE SMUDGE FIRE. Although insect repellents will generally keep mosquitos, black flies and other pests from biting, their buzzing near your eyes and ears can be very annoying. However, a good smudge fire can help keep insects away, and the smoke can add to your signal smoke.

Build the smudge ten or fifteen feet upwind from your camp. When coals have formed, throw on green or wet leaves or pine needles, moss, green evergreen boughs or any material that will not burn readily.

Types of Fire Lays

THE PYRAMID OR TEPEE. This fire lay is the quickest and simplest. It is good for boiling, making a bed of coals or for warmth. Once you have chosen your spot, scrape all forest litter back a safe distance. Place your tinder in the center, with the fine kindling put gently on top so as to not crush the tinder. The larger, more substantial pieces of wood should be placed in a circle, teepee-shaped, on top of the kindling.

When preparing this type of lay, you can use a "dingle-stick" over the fire. A dingle stick is nothing more than a green sapling sharpened at the butt. It is shoved into the ground and angled over a rock support so that its tip hovers over the fire. The pot or container is hung on this end by its handle. Its height is regulated by varying the distance of the supporting rock from the fire.

THE HUNTER LAY. This type of fire lay is used by many outdoorsmen in a hurry. It is constructed by laying two rows of rocks parallel and six to eight inches apart to support cooking utensils, building the fire in between. If there are no rocks handy, use two green logs about six to eight inches in diameter for supports. In either case, build the lay parallel with the wind. Draft can be regulated be placing different size rocks in front on the windy side.

A well-prepared fire is lighted.

THE PRAIRIE LAY. This type should be used on windy days. It keeps the sparks and fire in the hole where they belong. The hole should be about a foot deep, and jnst wide enough to support cooking pots. The sod should be placed on the windward side to prevent dirt from being blown into the containers.

Cooking without Utensils

In many cases a survivor doesn't have utensils to cook his food in, so he has to improvise. Here are a few methods that can be used with success.

ROASTING. This can be done in the coals of your campfire. You can coat fish, birds, freshwater mussels and many other foods with a layer of mud or clay and

Various fire lays: at top, a reflector fire, useful in front of lean-tos, and a log platform fire. At bottom, three varieties of cooking fires, with three placements of pots.

roast them directly in the flames or coals of a fire. Using this method, you won't lose food by burning it.

You need not pick off the feathers of fowl or scale fish prepared in this manner; just peel off the scales and feathers with the baked clay or mud when your food is thoroughly cooked.

PIT COOKING. Small food such as small bird's eggs, freshwater snails or any other shellfish may be cooked in quantity in a pit beneath your fire.

Fill a small, shallow pit with the food to be cooked. Line the pit or wrap the food in green plant leaves or cloth to keep the food clean. Next, cover the pit with a ¼" to ½-inch layer of sand or soil. Build your fire directly over it. After sufficient cooking (that will depend on the type of food and size), rake away the fire and recover the food.

STEAMING WITH HEATED STONES. This is the old "clambake" style, and it really works. Heat a number of stones in your fire, then allow the fire to burn down to the coals. Place such foods as freshwater mussels (in their shells) directly on and between the stones and cover the whole with plant leaves, grass or seaweed. Cover this with a layer of sand or soil. When thoroughly steamed in their own juices, clams, oysters and mussels will show a gaping open shell when uncovered. The food may then be eaten without further preparation.

Caution! Sometimes stones and rocks taken from stream beds or the water's edge will explode when placed in a fire. Try to obtain rocks inshore.

STONE BOILING. Fill a big bowl (if you have one) with water and food. Add red-hot stones until the water boils. Cover for at least an hour with large green leaves until the food is properly cooked.

STICK METHOD. You can also cook by the stick method, cutting any wild meat, tubers or roots into two inch squares or cubes, and lacing them on a green stick or limb. Broil or roast them over hot coals.

7

Living Off the Land: Plants

Throughout the world there are more than 300,000 classified plants. Of this vast number, more than 120,-000 varieties are edible. No one can possibly begin to identify or remember what all these plants look like, although many Boy Scouts and survival experts have a good working knowledge of many of the species found in North America. And there is no valid reason why, with a little field practice, you cannot do the same.

You should learn to identify at least a dozen or more of the most common plants found at various elevations in the woods, mountains and in deserts while you are hunting, fishing or while on one of your vacation jaunts. Take along a Boy Scout handbook or one of the little Golden regional guidebooks or nature guides. These books are a good value and are available all over the country. Books like *The American Southwest, The Pacific Northwest* and *The Weather* tell in colored pictures about each region, the types of plants, trees, birds and animals, where they live and how they are located.

The quickest and best methods to learn about wild plants is to have some experienced person point them out to you. Each time you are shown a plant, don't just make a mental note, but jot down its characteristics, and where and at what general elevation it was found. Learn to recognize vegetation patterns in tropical areas, deserts and cold regions.

The same plants, or some very similar in appearance, are found in other sections of the world at the same elevations. Some will vary only in minor detail. In temperate and tropical zones plants or fruits can be obtained the year around. In the subarctic and polar regions plant foods are usually found only during the short summer growing period. Nevertheless, in winter if you see dry plant stalks above the ground in windswept areas, be sure to dig and see if there are tubers or edible roots underneath.

With over 120,000 wilderness plants to choose from, there is no need to suffer from hunger, although some plants are tastier and more palatable than others. Plants are more common and easier to obtain than trapping wild animals, so use them as much as you can.

Under survival conditions wild plant and animal food will probably alter your diet almost completely. Your intestinal tract will probably change for a few days due to so much roughage. You may have dysentery or some type of diarrhea or your bowels may not move regularly until your system becomes accustomed to such a drastic change in diet. Don't worry; in a few days you will be all right.

You should have some practical knowledge of poisonous plants—where they grow and how to use them. Very few are deadly when eaten in small amounts (except poisonous fungi). Descriptions of wild plants are difficult to give, whether in line drawings or in words. On the following pages I have attempted to give general indications as to what edible as against poisonous plants look like.

WARNING. Never eat large quantities of strange plants without testing them first. Prepare a cooked sample, then take a mouthful, chew it, hold it in your mouth for five minutes. If it still tastes good, go ahead and eat it. If it tastes disagreeable, don't eat it. Generally, an unpleasant taste does not, in itself, necessarily mean poison, but a burning, nauseating, or bitter taste is a warning!

Starchy Foods

Many plants store large quantities of edible starch in their underground parts. Here are a few common plants.

TUBERS. Tubers of the wild potato with foliage similar to domestic cultivated varieties are edible. They are found mostly in tropical America. The tubers of water lilies and other plants such as cattails and tropical yams are abundant in tropical sections of Florida and Mexico, as well as parts of the north.

ROOTSTALKS. Rootstalks are found in many plants.

BULBS. Bulbs are produced most commonly by members of the lily family, such as the true lily, onion, tulip, daffodil. Many bulbs are edible.

Tubes, rootstalks and bulbs are a fine source of food because they are usually available throughout the year in most regions. The young stems of breadfruit contain plenty of starch.

Preparation

Raw starch is very difficult to digest, so all starchy food must be cooked. As a matter of fact, most edible wild foods taste bitter unless cooked. The first water should be drained off and the plants recooked in fresh water. The second cooking makes them more tender and tasty.

Vegetables

Vegetables are produced mostly from succulent leaves, pods, seeds, stems and nonwoody roots. Select only young tender kinds, but cook all vegetables.

PUFFBALLS. These are white to brownish in color and almost round in shape. In their edible stage the interior is full of pure white flesh. The puffball in this state may be fried or used as flavoring in wild game stew or soup. They are generally found on the ground in open meadows.

MUSHROOMS. Mushrooms are the *only* fungi that have fishlike gills. Mushrooms are usually found on the ground. In rare cases they may be found on decaying wood, down logs in forests or meadows. A large percentage are edible.

How to distinguish edible from poisonous mushrooms

Personally, I say don't take a chance unless you are *absolutely* certain you know the edible mushroom from the deadly one. Color is not a reliable guide in distinguishing poisonous from nonpoisonous mushrooms.

The deadly kinds, mostly aminitas, have certain characteristics in common. Poisonous mushrooms have a frill or ring (veil) around the upper part of the stem plus a cup (volva) at the base into which the stem fits (usually just below the ground level or covered with decaying forest litter). A few edible mushrooms sometimes have the frill or ring, but *never* the cup. Personally, I leave them alone. I just won't take a chance. Sometimes a mushroom that looks like an edible one because it doesn't have a cup may be deadly. The cup may have broken off.

When picking young mushrooms, don't mistake them for young puffballs, which are edible but without gills and central stem. To be certain, cut the young "button" vertically and look for gills and cup. If you find a poisonous one (always with gills), remember that cooking will *not* destroy the poisonous contents. Discard all suspected kinds at once.

ARROWHEAD. Sometimes it is called arrowleaf because of its pointed leaves. It is found in the wetlands and swamps or marshy areas from the Gulf of Mexico to central Canada. The starchy root is edible and may be prepared by boiling or roasting.

BURDOCK. This plant is widely distributed through Canada and the United States. Its leaves resemble rhubarb leaves and it grows on long, tough fiber stems. The plant averages three to seven feet in height. When in bloom, it has numerous hooked flower heads. The roots of the burdock are edible during the first year of growth, as are the younger shoots. The roots may be boiled or roasted. The young shoots are better boiled and used as greens.

CAMAS. I personally do not recommend camas, unless you are able to distinguish the edible species from the death camas. The camas is a member of the lily family and grows primarily in the northwest United States and Canada. The western camas should not be confused with the death camas, which also grows in western and southwestern states.

CATTAILS. This plant is a member of the bullrush family and is found throughout temperate North America. It occurs in both fresh and saltwater marshes, along small shallow lakes and ponds and quiet stream banks. The plant grows from three to eight feet high, and is common in waterfowl terrain. The edible portion is the tuberous root, which is cooked as a vegetable, and is also used to thicken emergency soups.

CENTURY PLANT. This is a member of the cactus family, and is widely scattered over arid and desert areas of the southwest. The spiny plant grows to a height of three to eight feet or more, with a long pole-like stem that carries the blooming flowers. The spike-like spines may be cut away, leaving a bulby base that looks similar to an overgrown pineapple. To cook this vegetable, prepare it like a squash; it can be baked or roasted. I like it roasted.

CHICKORY. This plant is usually found in the eastern United States and Canada. Its root is often used as a coffee substitute. The root is also used as an herb.

CHOKECHERRY. This large slender shrub grows six to sixteen feet high. The shrub blooms with long, tapering stems having numerous small, white blossoms. The blossoms later are succeeded by tapering clusters of red berries, which turn black when ripe. The berries are very tart, but edible. This shrub grows in wide areas of the United States and Canada.

CHUFA. Chufa is one of the grasses, having a bearded tuber root system. It is scattered across Canada, and southward into the tropics. The tubers may be roasted or boiled as a pot vegetable, or roasted and beaten into wilderness flour, which will thicken soups. The tubes may be rolled in wet green leaves and roasted in the coals of your campfire. The wet leaves prevent the tubers from burning.

CLOVER. Various parts of clover can be used as an emergency survival food. The dried heads can be pounded and used as a bread food. The young tender leaves can be used as part of a salad or cooked as an herb.

DANDELION. This is one of the most widely distributed wild plants on the North American continent. Everyone is familiar with its jagged pointed leaves and bright yellow composite flower. The stem, when broken, bleeds a milky bitter fluid. The young plants make good greens but are somewhat bitter. They should be boiled and the water drained off, then cooked again until tender. The greens then taste somewhat like spinach. (Note: this is one plant with a bitter milky fluid that *is* safe to eat.)

DOCK. There are over a dozen species of dock, scattered over most of temperate North America. The young leaves are used as herbs or as greens. Most species of dock are short, stout plants with leaves from six to twelve inches long growing out of stout leafstalks. The leaves are elongated. Dock thrives near swamps and marshy areas. Its range is southward from Canada over temperate sections of the States.

FIREWEED. This plant gets its name because it grows up quickly after forest fires in North America. It grows approximately four to six feet tall, and is characterized by bright, lavender-colored flowers. The raw shoots are cooked as a pot vegetable. The pith from the mature stalks can be made into soup.

HOG PEANUT. Similar to the groundnut, the hog peanut grows with a long, twining vine, and has underground fruits in tough pods. These pods are boiled, which softens the skins so the seed can be removed. The seeds are cooked like dry beans. Hog peanuts grow from southern Canada to the Gulf of Mexico.

INDIAN CUCUMBER. This plant has a long, slender stem, with a circle of several leaves branching out from the stem near the top. At the top is a smaller circle with fewer leaves near which are black-purple berries. The root is a small tuber about one inch in diameter. This part can be eaten raw. Indian cucumbers are common in eastern Canada southward to Florida.

JERUSALEM ARTICHOKE. A member of the sunflower family, this plant is native to portions of central North America. It has a tuber root similar to the Irish potato's. This is the edible part. It may be boiled, baked, roasted or eaten raw.

LICHENS. These tiny plants grow on rocks, and as emergency food have saved many lives. When boiled, the substance forms into jellylike food.

MALLOW. Mallow is found in most areas of the United States and Canada. The young plants may be boiled and used as greens.

MARSH MARIGOLD. Sometimes called American Cowslip, marigold is one of the buttercup family plants. It ranges from the subarctic zone to the Gulf states. The flower has a bright yellow, waxy looking bloom. The edible part is the plant's top, and only the tender tips should be used. Prepare them by double boiling, draining off the first water. Use as pot herbs or greens. *Caution:* Do not eat the plant in its raw state! It is poisonous!

MILKWEED. There are forty or more varieties of the common milkweed. The plant is light green in color, and grows to a height of three or four feet. When the stem or leaves are broken, the plant bleeds a bitter milky fluid similar to the dandelion. The young shoots are edible just after they emerge from the soil. These are prepared like other greens. Although this plant exudes a bitter, milky fluid, it is not poisonous.

MOUNTAIN SORREL. This plant is scattered throughout the States and Canada. It is small, with rounded leaves, resembling a small rhubarb plant. Years ago, when sailors and explorers were forced to eat salt meats, it was eaten to prevent scurvy; a common name for it is scurvy grass. It is prepared as other greens are.

MUSTARD. The common yellow mustard plants are native to many regions in the States. The plant grows to a height of three or four feet. The young plant leaves are edible. Under emergency conditions, you may be happy that this plant is readily available most of the year.

PIGWEED. Called lamb's quarters in some areas pigweed grows throughout the temperate zones of North America. The plant grows to six or eight feet. The young leaves are used as greens.

POKEWEED. This perennial herb has large petioled leaves, by which I mean that the leaf and stalk are in combination. The plant reaches a height of four to eight feet. It is plentiful in Canada and the United States.

Pokeweed blooms with a white flower, which is succeeded by purple berries. The roots of the plant are large and branching; they are poisonous and should never be eaten. Only the young shoots are safe to eat. They are prepared like other greens.

SORREL. There are several species of sorrel, which is often mistaken for small dock. It grows principally in eastern Canada. The plant is used as an herb. It is good to nibble on to stop the hunger pangs, and it will help quench thirst.

SUNFLOWER. This plant is common to the Great Plains regions of the States and southern Canada. The seeds are nutritious and are useful in making wilderness flour. They are usually baked, and the seeds are removed and shelled.

WATERCRESS. This is a plant that can be picked and eaten at once. It is aquatic and its leaves grow above the water surface. A member of the mustard family, the plant grows in clear springs and streams in the temperate zones in the hills and mountains of North America.

WILD ONION. The plant grows with a thin straight stem and has long slender leaves. The flower bloom occurs at the tip of the stem. This plant is readily recognized by its strong garliclike odor and flavor. The small bulb from which the plant grows is the edible portion. Much of the strong odor and taste can be dispelled by boiling. Pour the first water off and boil again until it is soft. It flavors other wild foods well.

WILD PARSNIP. Unless you can distinguish wild parsnip from the deadly water hemlock, I recommend that you leave this plant strictly alone. The two plants look very similar.

A FEW MORE HELPFUL WILD FOODS. Wild rose hips (these have pods containing seeds surrounded by fruit), yarrow, peavine (sometimes called vetch, false solomon's seal, beebalm, horsetail and yarrow). No need to starve! Remember, almost any fruit you see birds eating is usually safe to eat.

Seaweeds as Food

Many seaweeds are edible, but never eat too much of them at a time. Large amounts of seaweed are violently purgative, and cause general weakness, but none are actually poisonous. They may be eaten in small portions and used as flavoring in other foods. All seaweeds are rich in iodine, minerals and vitamins. They will also prevent scurvy. Some have too much lime carbonate or are too bony and rough to eat. Many are covered with slime.

The coarse, dark green seaweed with large air bladders is called rockweed. It has no food value, but in and underneath it you will usually find small crabs, shrimp and shellfish. It is excellent for temporarily wrapping shellfish.

When collecting seaweed for food, do not take plants stranded on the beach; choose only plants attached to rocks or those floating free in the water.

Tree Bark

The cambium or inner bark (between the wood and bark) can be stripped off and eaten. Trees with edible bark are generally familiar to most vacationers, and are quite easy to identify. All pines, willows, birth, aspen, cottonwood are edible.

Edible Nuts

Edible nuts are the most sustaining of all raw foods, and are found throughout the world. Many American nut trees such as oaks, hickories, hazelnuts and beech-nuts, are widely distributed throughout the North Temperate Zone. Familiarity with some of the common North American nut trees will help you locate nut-bearing trees in other regions.

Several species of evergreen trees, such as sugar pine, coulter pine, yellow pine and pinion pine, produce edible pine nuts. To remove the seeds, bake or roast the cone. This will force open the cone and the seeds can be shaken out. Usually, when the cones are ripe, the seeds can be shaken out by striking them against a rock. To keep from getting pitch all over your hands, hold the cone with a piece of cloth or pound a sharpened stick into the pine cone and then strike it with a rock.

How to Test Plants for Edibility

Some plants are poisonous enough to cause severe sickness, skin irritation, blindness, paralysis or even death. The following precautions and tips should help you in determining what to eat:

- Unless you are desperate, select only plants you know or resemble vegetation which you are familiar with.
- Use caution. Put a small raw portion of the plant selected into your mouth and chew it. Don't swallow it! Spit it out and wait to see if there are any ill effects in the mouth or to the tongue.
- If no ill effects follow initial experimentation, eat a small portion and wait to see if you have any reaction. If not, cook some of the plant and eat it. If no illness occurs after waiting six to eight hours, it is probably safe.
- If you discover signs of poisoning (headache, dizziness, nausea, weakness, blurred vision or vomiting) act *immediately!* Drink lots of water, then stick your finger down your throat and vomit it up.

Skin Irritants

The few poisonous plants that act as skin irritants all belong to the same natural family. These contact poisonous plants are the poisons oak, ivy and sumac. They are extremely variable plants and may occur as ground vines, climbing vines or shrubs. They are widely distributed in hedgerows, thickets and woods throughout the country.

Unfortunately, poison oak and poison ivy are not always easily recognized, and poison sumac is even more difficult to avoid in brushy or swampy habitat.

POISON IVY AND POISON OAK. The leaves of poison ivy and oak vary greatly in size and texture, so a person accustomed to recognizing these plants in one section of the country often will not recognize them in another. It is helpful, however, to remember that poison ivy is woody in older plants and, like the poison oak, each leaf is divided into three separate leaflets. The fruiting plants bear a cluster of small white berries.

POISON SUMAC. This is a tall shrub or small tree. Each leaf is composed of seven or more (sometimes ten or twelve) leaflets arranged along a conspicuously red central axis, with one leaflet at the pointed edges. The latter is an important factor that distinguishes poison sumac from its nonpoisonous species.

If you come in contact with these plants, use strong soap *immediately,* or use the poison oak remedy in your first aid or survival kit. Generally, if you do not take action within five to ten minutes, it is too late and you will have to suffer with the burning itch for days.

Desert Plants

Many of the over 200 desert plants native to the United States and Mexico are edible. Listed here are a few of the most common and easiest to identify:

Young cactus and prickly pear are very good once the spines are removed. I burn off the spines and scrape or peel the fruit. Don't handle any desert cactus without gloves! I usually spear the fruit with a sharp stick once I have cut it from the main stalk and roast it over a fire until the spines are burnt enough to scrape or the pear peeled. The fruit of the saguaro is edible if you can get at it. So are the fruit and meat of the beavertail and other cacti. In fact, most all flowers of desert and other plants are edible.

The fruits of Englemann's pear and the bud of the stalk of the century plant are edible. Don't overlook the desert gourd; it is a member of the squash family. It trails along the ground just like the domestic squash.

The seeds of desert or Utah serviceberry, Gamble oak and ironwood are nourishing as are the nuts of the desert pinion pine. Desert Indian tribes enjoy eating the seeds of mesquite and jojoba.

Don't eat mescalbean or coralbean, identified by their bright red seeds. These plants are poisonous. They grow to five feet tall, are stout and stocky and have glossy green leaves and flowers similar to domestic wisteria. The woody seed pods contain three to four red seeds. You can't eat mescalbeans, but you can eat the stalk or shoot parts. The leaves may be cut for moisture.

Plant Foods in Tropical Areas

In tropical areas like Florida, Hawaii, Mexico and the Pacific islands the tender shoots of bamboo, nuts and fruits of coconut, sago, buri, rattan, assai, piva, patawn and bacaba palms are edible. (It will be wise to go to your local library and look up these exotic tropical plants if you are planning a trip to the Pacific islands. (Also, see chapter on Jungle Survival.)

Preparing Wild Food

Generally, boil plant roots and tubers. Seeds can be used to make broth or soup if seaweed or meat is added. In the tropics, however, some tubers (such as taro and manioc) must be soaked or boiled in water to remove harmful substances. This water cannot be used for broth.

To give taste to stews, add wild onions, puffballs, morels, succulent stems and leaves of plants for flavor.

To prepare seaweed, wash it in water, dry in sun on wood or on a rock or stone platform, pound when dry and sprinkle over food.

BOILING, ROASTING, BAKING AND FRYING. These are efficient methods of preparing wild foods. Cooking in a pit or clambake style is slower, but takes less attention and protects food from ever-present flies and other pests.

FRUITS. Succulent fruits are best boiled. Large, tough or heavy-skinned fruits are best baked or roasted.

POTHERBS (GREENS). Boiled leaves, stems and buds until tender. Several changes of water with subsequent rinsings will help eliminate bitter juices and undesirable tastes.

ROOTS AND TUBERS. These may also be boiled, but to me are tastier when baked or roasted.

NUTS. Most nuts can be eaten raw, but acorns are too bitter and must be cooked. Acorns should be boiled and the thick skin removed, then dried and eaten. Or you can boil them, adding some of the ashes from your fire to eliminate the tannin. The ashes should be washed off, and the nuts crushed and molded into small cakes and then baked.

GRAINS AND SEEDS. These should be parched (roasted) to make them tastier and more digestible.

MUSHROOMS. If you insist on eating mushrooms, cut them thin. The tender ones can be stewed slowly in about ten minutes. Thick, dry tough caps and stems require about forty minutes of stewing or they may be fried crisp. Fresh caps may be boiled or baked on hot stones or on a greased iron, two to five minutes to a side.

Drying Plant Food

Plant food can be dried by wind, air, sun or fire with or without smoke. Perhaps a combination of these methods may be necessary, depending on the weather and your particular situation. The main object is to get rid of all moisture.

Plantains, bananas, breadfruit, tubers, leaves, berries —in fact, most wild foodstuffs—can be dried.

A fire may be used if necessary. Edible mushrooms or other fungi can be dried in the sun or over a fire. They will keep for days if kept dry.

Pack a good supply of dried wild food with you while you travel to civilization, You will need it.

8

Living Off Animals and Fish

A knowledge of how to stalk or ambush game is a must for anyone placed in a survival situation for *any great length* of time. As mentioned before, animal food provides more food value per pound than any other food found in the wilderness. This is especially true if the animal is fat, so save all fat for cooking. If you kill a deer, elk or bear, you will have more meat than yon can possibly eat in a week.

This of course brings up a salient point: many outdoorsmen have never hunted, especially for big game, and are not particularly keen on doing so. These men and women quite naturally would not be carrying firearms along on their outdoor excursions. This is all well and good, but most of these same people are used to packing away each week several pounds of the good red meat that is so sanitarily wrapped at the local supermarket. They are used to getting their protein and fat in this form, and any major change in eating habits that occurs in the outdoors (where there are no white-coated butchers to perform the required butchery) may make them considerably less energetic and less able to deal with the pressing problems of survival.

Stalking game.

I am *not* going to take a stand in this book pro- or anti-hunting. I *am* going to urge the reader to peruse this chapter with an open mind, with a view toward the fact that the information it contains may be useful to those who are stuck in a survival situation for more than several days. Such a period of stress is simply not the time to become a vegetarian overnight. Therefore, you will have to know how to preserve the surplus by cooking, making jerky or by freezing it in a nearby snowbank. If temperatures are below freezing, the rest of the meat can be hung high out on a limber limb in a tree where bear and other animals cannot reach it. Generally, if a bear is in the territory, it will come to feed on the offal.

Tips on Stalking and Hunting Game

Warm-blooded animals are wary and must be stalked carefully. To hunt them requires skill and patience.

Stalking game when the woods are dry is most difficult. The dry forest cover crackles under each footstep, alerting all game and birds to the presence of an intruder. Sound carries far in the woods. Under these conditions it is wiser to build a blind from nearby shrubs so that you can ambush the animals. In this manner you save your strength and energy by letting the animals come to you.

Here are a few pointers on how to proceed:

• First look for animal sign. It is useless to hunt in a barren area. Find a place where animals pass: game trails, crossings, watering places where animal trails lead to a spring, stream or lake, feeding or bedding grounds. Look for fresh tracks and droppings—the fresher they are, the better your chances are of collecting meat.

• Generally animals head for water and forage at sunrise. As soon as they have eaten their fill, they head for a bedding ground or browse around until sunset, when they water and head for their night bedding grounds. On clear moonlight nights they are apt to feed off and on all night and bed down during the day. It is practically useless to hunt during a storm or heavy rain. Animals, like humans, seek shelter.

- The best time to hunt is in the very early morning or toward dusk. Game is more plentiful and more apt to be found near water, in forest clearings, meadows, ridge tops, passes or along the edges of thickets.

- Place your hideout downwind and hunt against the wind so that the animal can't smell you and "spook." Wait for the game to come within range. Remain motionless and quiet, until ready to fire. Be sure to pick your shot carefully. Don't waste precious ammunition or arrows.

- If you move along, as in stalking, be cautious, move slowly and as silently as you can. Most animals have keen sight and an excellent sense of smell. Try to see the game before it sights you.

- On topping a ridge, crawl up the last few yards to a lookout point and scan the area below you carefully, using brush or tall grass for concealment. Scan the area close by and then further out. Just move your eyes from side to side. If you move your head, do so very, very slowly. Game is attracted to movement more than color. Never silhouette yourself against the sky! Keep close to the ground and peek around a rock if no bushes are present. By being hidden in this manner you have an advantage over the animal.

- If game has sighted you but hasn't taken off, stop and freeze. Hold your position. Remain motionless until the animal lowers its head and starts to graze again. Stay quiet for a short period, then slowly back out of sight and stalk from another point keeping in mind to approach against the wind.

The Blood Trail

If your shot connects, but the animal takes off, check its blood trail. Blood may show on brush to leave a trail and indicate how high the wound is. Generally, a large-caliber slug makes a blood trail easy to follow.

Pinkish, foamy blood on the ground and splattered on nearby bushes indicates a lung hit. If bleeding heavily, the animal will not go far before collapsing. Search carefully for it. The animal may have fallen behind a rock or bush out of sight.

Red blood indicates a body hit. If not vitally wounded, game can travel far and may not recover, but you may lose it.

Dark or brownish-red generally means a gut shot. Such game can go far before dying slowly if not tracked down.

If you come on a wounded animal, approach it with caution.

If water is nearby, it might pay to move your bivouac camp to a location near where you killed your animal, to save time and energy.

About Bear

Bear usually will follow along game trails, but keep more or less clear of open meadows. Usually their droppings will be full of berry seeds such as manzanita. The dung will also contain hair from small animals

Building a deadfall for small animals.

they have eaten, such as ground squirrels. Their presence may be noted around where you have dressed out other animals. Other signs appear where the bear has been digging out ground squirrels or marmots. Unless you've had some experience in big-game hunting, keep away from bear.

Catching Birds

An easy way to catch a bird is to bait a fishhook. Be sure to tie the anchor end of the cord so the bird cannot take off. If birds are moulting, they may be run down and clubbed, speared, stoned or shot with

a gun or slingshot. However, it takes practice to hit
a bird or small animal with a slingshot. Too many outdoor writers make it sound easy, but it isn't.

GULLS AND SEA BIRDS. Gulls may also be caught
with gorge and line. A gorge is a small stick about the
diameter of a narrow pencil, sharpened at each end.
It is notched in the center and a fish line is attached.
When baited, it is left on the beach or let out on the
water on a float or piece of wood. Be sure to stake the
beach end securely, since a duck or seagull or other
large sea bird will put up quite a struggle, and they
are quite strong.

Small Game

Rabbits are usually the easiest to catch. They often
run in circles, returning to the same area from which
they were frightened. If you shoot, aim for the head,
otherwise you will spoil most of the meat. If the animal
is running, of course, you can't take a chance and waste
ammunition, so, aim at the whole body. *And,* don't
forget to lead the animal a yard or so, if he is really
moving fast! Sometimes if you whistle, the rabbit may
stop long enough to look back. Then drop him.

Desert Animals

Some writers say most desert animals are scarce.
I have been stationed in several desert areas and I do
not agree with this. Naturally, since their presence depends upon water and vegetation, there are few animals
in bare sand areas.

You will normally find animals near water holes, in
grassy desert canyons, low-lying areas or river beds.
Animals live where some moisture is available, under

rocks, at desert wells (where rain water collects in rock depressions) and in the shade of desert bushes.

They hole up during the heat of the day and then prowl for food toward evening and at night. The most common animals are small rodents, rabbits, prairie dogs, rats, desert fox, coyote and desert sheep.

In the high plateau deserts snakes and lizards are usually plentiful. Rodents may be caught by finding their burrows and trapping them with a loop snare,

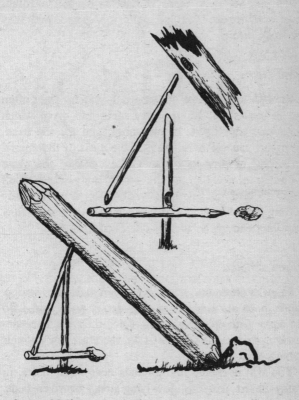

A deadfall with a "figure-4" trigger.

A deadfall and a drag snare in combination.

trap or deadfall when they come out at dusk or dawn. You can also find occasional land snails under rocks or bushes. Anything that creeps, crawls, swims, runs or flies is generally safe to eat. Insects are full of protein. They are best eaten when roasted.

Snares That Work

Primitive snares operate on one of the following principles: Catching the animal in a sliding loop, or drop-

A twitch-up trigger snare.

ping a rock or log weight heavy enough to pin down or kill an animal.

All snares and deadfalls should be simple to make and easy to operate, otherwise you will be wasting precious time that could be put to better use by gathering plant food.

Snares and deadfalls should be adjusted to hair-trigger performance. Loops for the snares can be made from boot laces, strong cord or any wire available. However, stiff steel wire makes the best loops for grabbing small game.

Don't waste time and energy in placing snares or deadfalls in animal runways unless there are fresh tracks or other spoor such as fresh droppings indicating that the trail is being used.

Hanging Snares

The hanging or "twitch-up," sometimes called a spring-pole by trappers, is simple to make. While the deadfall is good for killing small game, there is no one trap that fits all requirements. Some animals may shy away from a deadfall for some reason, but fall victim to a hanging snare.

Rock or Log Deadfall

A flat slab of rock generally works better than a log. Otherwise you will have to cut a log that's green and heavy enough to do the job. There are two types of triggers that work best for deadfalls, the figure-four and the three-pin trigger as shown in the drawings.

Location of Trap Sets

Where you place a deadfall or snare, of course, depends on the species of game you are trying to catch. If you are attempting to kill a bear or deer, you will have to use a heavy log large enough to hold or kill the beast. Naturally it will have to be set in a bear or deer runway. For smaller game, a "twitch-up" will do. Check along streams for fresh signs and for animal dens. Where a stream branches off from the main fork is another good place to make a "set." Whenever there are cliffs or rocky banks further up a small stream, such spots, especially if there are dens nearby, are excellent places to set a deadfall and some snare traps.

As mentioned before, of all the small animals, the rabbit is easiest to snare. The snare or deadfall may be baited with wild fruit, succulent plants or roots. For other small game, bait the trap with whatever you have or can find. Fish entrails, lizards, snakes, frogs, grasshoppers, will do. Remember, if a bear is in the area, he usually will come at night to feed on any animals you have dressed out. If you have firearms, ambush him, but be sure that you are on the right or left from the direction of the wind so that the smell of the offal is stronger than your scent.

If All Else Fails

If you are unable to secure game with firearms, snares or deadfalls—*don't give up*. There is no need to starve. If the going really gets tough, there is high protein food in pinebark beetles and their larva which have a nutty pine needle flavor. For beetles and larva, look for pine trees that have faded to light yellow needles indicating that the tree has been girdled by bark beetles and is dying. Chop or break off strips of bark to obtain the larva and adult pine beetles.

Roast grasshoppers, lizards and snakes are not bad to eat. Remove the heads of snakes and lizards, and

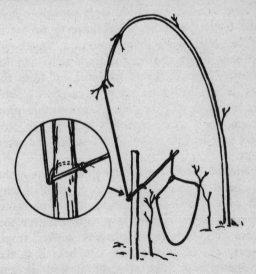

A small-animal twitch-up.

A spring-up snare, which can be made from fish line, shoelaces, etc.

dress by removing the entrails, then roast over a bed of coals. Roast the grasshoppers first, then break off the wings and legs; the rest is edible. With some green plants, root and wild berry food, you should be able to keep your strength up and travel far, if you decide to walk out.

Fish—Where to Find Them

You may be able to add fish to your survival food list.

Bass (largemouth)	Warm lakes, ponds, rivers and in weed and lily beds. *June–Sept.*
Bass (smallmouth)	Cold clear lakes, ponds, streams, near or over rock shoals. *June–Sept.*

Bluegill	Rivers, lakes, ponds or weed-beds to 10 ft. depth. *May–Oct.*
Bullhead	Most all waters, mud bottoms, near weedbeds. *May–Oct.*
Carp	Lakes, ponds, slow streams and rivers, weeds and mud bottoms. *May–Aug.*
Catfish	Slow moving rivers, lakes, ponds, weed bottoms. *May–Oct.*
Crappie	Near docks, pilings, weeds, lakes, streams, ponds. *May–Sept.*
Muskellunge	Large lakes, rivers, in weeds, in shade of logs and docks. *May–Sept.*
Perch (yellow)	Lakes, ponds, near weeds, lillies, logs. *All year.*
Pike (northern)	Slow rivers, lakes, ponds, near weeds, etc. *May–Sept.*
Trout	Cold lakes, streams, rivers. *May–Oct.*

These are the best months to have the best luck. However, some type of fish can usually be caught all year in most wild areas.

To Clean the Fish

1. Scale fish thoroughly.

2. Cut with tip of knife along dorsal and belly fins. Deep enough to lift fins out with bones attached.

3. To gut fish, cut from throat to vent and clean cavity thoroughly. Fry or bake over coals or sun-

dry for future use. Saltwater shellfish can be eaten raw, but it is safer to cook them. Turtle eggs can be boiled or roasted. Most people prefer them roasted. I know from experience that I do.

Dressing out Your Kill

All game, large or small, should be at least field dressed (sometimes referred to as hog-dressed) as soon as possible after having been shot or trapped.

Insert a knife at point of brisket and cut forward toward the head, turning the animal with its head downhill so that it will bleed freely.

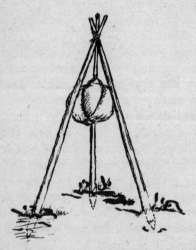

A simple method of preserving food above the reach of most animals.

If you have a container, drain all the blood possible into it. The blood will help with soup or at least give you some excellent food value. You can't be squeamish under survival conditions. The blood will only keep for a short period, so use it quickly.

Next, open the carcass from crotch to throat, being very careful not to puncture the intestines, bladder or pauch; if you have a belt ax, use it on the breastbone. On all operations prevent hair from coming into contact with the meat. Cut around the anal vent and sex organs in the pelvic cavity. (I usually tie these off so that they don't leak.) Now turn the carcass with the head downhill. Cut windpipe and gullet free at throat. A small knife is best. (You are apt to cut your fingers with a large knife in this confined space.) Hold these in your hand and pull backward, at the same time cutting free from the carcass any part that tends to hold. Remove all internal organs at the base of tail.

Open the chest cavity by spreading it with a stick or two. Drain off all surplus blood and wipe clean with leaves or a cloth.

Do not wash with water. It will sour meat quickly. When wiping inside of carcass, blood smears the inside and will dry and glaze over the inside. This helps to preserve the meat.

The carcass should be removed to a shady spot to cool out. It is safe to eat the liver, kidneys and heart any time. The rest of the meat should cure for a week or so, but under survival conditions, can be eaten any time. It may give you diarrhea for a day or so, but you may need nourishment to give you strength to carry on, so eat it.

Cut away surplus fat to be used when you fry meat. Otherwise leave it on roasts.

Dressing out Small Animals

Small animals such as rabbits, squirrels (both tree and ground), marmots, skunks, porcupine, woodchucks and others are dressed out the same way as larger ones.

If you don't need the fur for any reason, I find the quickest way to skin rabbits and other small game is to pinch up the fur in the middle of the back, cut it open and peel off like a glove, pulling with one hand toward the head and the other toward the tail. Then cut the hide loose from the legs and tail.

Caution must be used when cooking wild game to see that it is thoroughly cooked. Some animals like those of the deer family (deer, elk and moose) have liver flukes. If the liver is very light or very dark and spotted, it is possible that the liver is contaminated. Nevertheless, if it is well cooked, you can eat it in emergency situations. Rabbits, deer and bear are sometimes contaminated with the larva of trichinosis or tularemia.

If the meat is well cooked there is no threat of contracting the diseases. However, if you nick your skin while dressing out the animal, wash your hands thoroughly as soon as possible.

Leave any sick looking or very slow-moving animal alone. It may be contaminated with one of the sicknesses mentioned above.

Preserving Your Kill

If the animal has been trapped or shot some distance from your emergency camp, it might be well to quarter the carcass and pack it there. Otherwise, move your camp as near to your kill as possible.

Once you have killed a big-game animal and enjoyed

your first meal from it, preserving the rest of the carcass presents quite a problem.

However, there are several methods of doing this. The meat can be cooked and part of it placed in a primitive improvised cooler by digging a pit approximately two feet deep and two feet wide. The cooler should be lined with rocks or leaves, and the meat wrapped in cloth or leaves with the top covered with boughs or whatever is at hand. If there is a snow bank nearby, the cooked or raw meat can be wrapped and buried in nature's freezer. The third method is to dry the meat.

Making Jerky

The above advice is generally suggested for permanent camps when one stays in one spot and waits for rescue. If you are walking out, it is better to make as much jerky from the rest of the meat ~ you can carry.

Most meat can be preserved by drying or making jerky over a slow fire or in hot sun. This can be accomplished by cutting the meat into thin strips about one inch in diameter. Next take a stone and pound each strip of meat on a rock to tenderize it. If you have salt or any other seasoning, pound it into the meat, then hang the results on a fishline, wire, rope or green limb out of reach of animals where the sun and wind can dry-cure the strips.

To keep blow-flies, yellowjackets and other pests away, build a smoky fire underneath the drying rack. The smoke will assist in curing and flavoring the meat.

Fish also can be cleaned, split open and dried in this manner. This will solve your food transportation problem. You can travel for weeks on nothing but jerked meat, and when supplemented with some plant food along the way, there is no need to starve.

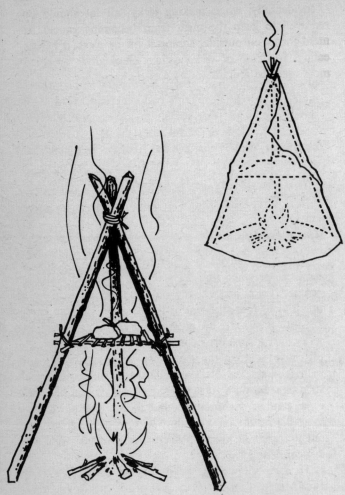

How to smoke meat or fish: three poles about 7 feet in length form a tripod. Tie a green-wood grate about 4 feet above the ground. Spread the food out on this grate. Build a fire of green, nonpitchy wood. As indicated at top, cover tripod tepee fashion with cloth, but close it tight at top and sides.

Incidentally, when making jerky, all fat should be removed to keep the meat from becoming rancid. If mold forms on outside, scrape it off or wash it before eating. In damp or wet weather, smoked or air-dried meat must be redried to prevent molding.

To preserve meat, recook it once each day. This is especially important in warm weather.

Preserving Fish

Use a knapsack or any other type of sack or bag to carry extra food picked up along the way during the day. Wrap soft berries or fruit in leaves to keep them intact.

Carry shellfish, crabs and shrimp in wet seaweed. Always clean fish immediately; wash them well and carry them on a line or branch pole. Excess fish can be slit. Cut off the head and gut it and remove the backbone. Spread it apart, and cut it thin. Dry it over a smoky fire or spread it on hot rocks, or hang from branches in the sun to cure in wind and sun. If sea water is available, splash some of it on the fish to salt the outside. Do not eat shellfish that has died. It must be cooked alive.

9

Woodlore

Rafting Rivers

Rafting down rivers is one of the oldest known modes of travel, and under survival conditions it is often the best and quickest way to reach civilization. In building a raft it is best to use dry, dead, standing trees. Spruce makes the best raft, but any handy dry trees or dry down logs will do.

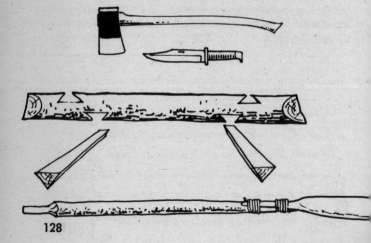

Raft for fast water. If you have to shoot rapids to get out of the wilderness, your raft should have cross pieces lashed as above so it will not break up. Bind the logs with rope or vines, using diagonal lashings.

You can learn by watching an experienced woodsman use this important tool, and by following safe ax practice as outlined in the illustrations.

Safety Tips

Always keep an ax or other sharp-edged tools masked by keeping them in a leather sheath or wrapping the cutting edge in canvas or burlap when not in use.

Always warm the ax blade in cold weather to keep from chipping the blade.

Avoid cutting knots in wood; they can chip the edge of the blade. Always cut around knots. They can also cause an ax to glance and cause an accident.

When carrying an unmasked ax, grip the handle close to the head and carry it with the cutting edge pointed down, or away from the body. If you stumble or fall, you can throw it away from you.

The ax should be carried on the downhill side when contouring steep terrain.

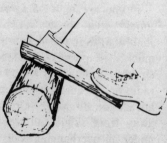

Using the axe. The left column is the correct way, at right is the wrong way. Top, cutting off branches; middle, cutting up logs; bottom, splitting logs.

Knots—Lashings—Hitches

Anyone traveling the wilderness trails should know how to tie a few simple knots, lashings and hitches. A number of these are shown in the following illustrations:

All campers should know how to tie a square knot, a bowline, a half-hitch, a clove hitch and to splice a rope.

Thunder and Lightning

Lightning is actually a gigantic electrical spark. It is most visible when it surges from earth to cloud or cloud to earth, although lightning can also travel between clouds or within them. The air turbulence that forms a storm cloud separates electrical forces inside the cloud itself. Negative electrical forces accumulate in the lower portions of the cloud, and positive electrical forces concentrate in the cloud's upper area as well as on the ground below. Like magnets, opposites attract each other. Consequently, in a series of steps, lightning crosses through the air to bridge the gaps between these forces.

If you are in a boat, get off the water. Swimmers should seek shelter. Hikers and mountain climbers should go to lower elevation, away from high points as quickly as possible. Lightning generally travels from cloud to ground, but a high peak, ridge, tall tree, tower, radio or TV antenna or steel fishing rod on a boat, can attract the discharge. Go into heavy timber, but stay away from single tall trees. If possible, seek shelter under an overhanging rock or cave.

Thunder is the explosive noise caused by the heating and expanding of air in the path of the lightning's millions of volts. The sound itself is harmless.

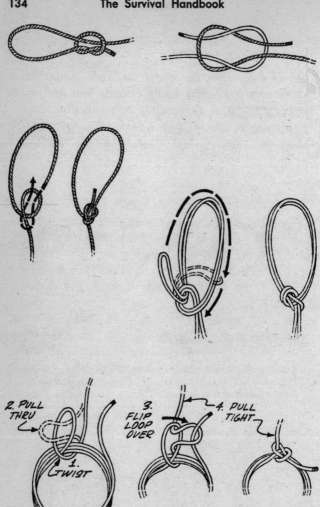

A collection of useful knots: Top to bottom, left to right, they are Slip Knot, Reef or Square Knot, Bowline, Bowline on a Bight, Bowline on a Coil.

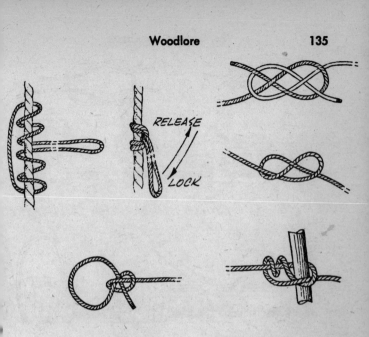

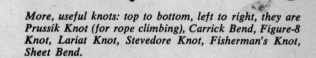

More, useful knots: top to bottom, left to right, they are Prussik Knot (for rope climbing), Carrick Bend, Figure-8 Knot, Lariat Knot, Stevedore Knot, Fisherman's Knot, Sheet Bend.

How to Ascertain Lightning Storm Distance

Since the speed of light is approximately a million times faster than the speed of sound, there is a delay between the lightning flash and the accompanying thunderclap. The distance between you and the storm can

CLOVE HITCH · SLIPPERY CLOVE HITCH · TIMBER HITCH · KILLICK HITCH

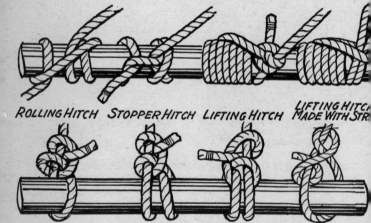

ROLLING HITCH · STOPPER HITCH · LIFTING HITCH · LIFTING HITCH MADE WITH STR.

TWO HALF HITCHES · ROUND TURN AND TWO HALF HITCHES · FISHERMAN'S BEND · STUDDING SAIL TACK BEND OR BUNTLINE HITCH

STUDDING SAIL HALYARD BEND · TOPSAIL HALYARD BEND · TOPSAIL SHEET BEND · MARLINSPIKE HITCH

KNOTS USED TO FORM ONE OR MORE LOOPS

BOWLINE **RUNNING BOWLINE** **BOWLINE ON A BIGHT** **FRENCH BOWL**

SPANISH BOWLINE **FISHERMAN'S EYE** **CRABBER'S EYE** **OPENHAND KNO**

MIDSHIPMAN'S HITCH **JUG SLING OR HACKAMORE** **TOMFOOLS KNOT** **JURY MAST HEA**

KNOTS USED TO SHORTEN ROPE

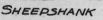

SHEEPSHANK **KNOTTED SHEEPSHANK**

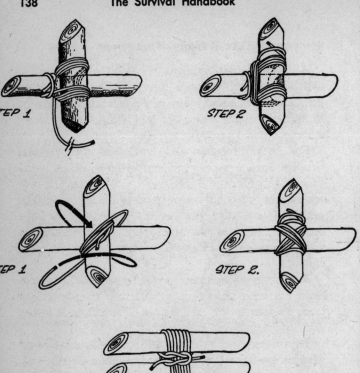

STEP 1

STEP 2

STEP 1

STEP 2.

There are several types of lashings. Top, the square lashing is used for tying two poles together at right angles. Middle, the diagonal lashing is used to spring two spars together. Bottom, the shear lashing is used when constructing shear logs or a tripod for a tepee.

be computed by counting the number of seconds between lightning flash and report of thunder and dividing by five. This is the number of miles between you and the storm.

Measures to Take in Heavy Windstorms

All major windstorms can represent a threat to life and property, but the most dangerous ones are tornadoes and hurricanes. Many of the precautions against tornadoes and hurricanes can be utilized for any windstorm.

For both tornadoes and hurricanes the National Weather Service issues two alerts to the public. A hurricane or tornado *watch* identifies specific areas where a tornado or hurricane may develop during a specific period of time, or where one is close enough to be a threat of danger within twenty-four hours. Persons in such areas should begin at once to think of safety precautions.

A tornado or hurricane *warning* means that a tornado has been sighted or a hurricane is approaching land. Persons in the affected areas should take immediate precautions as outlined below.

Tornadoes are the most violent and destructive of all windstorms. Typically, tornadoes are short-lived storms with winds rotating at very high speeds. They descend to the ground in a frightening, funnel-shaped cloud from thunderstorm cloud systems. The destructive action of the tornado is produced by the combined force of the strong revolving winds and the reduced pressure near the center of the funnel. Buildings collapse and windows explode. They appear frequently in the midwestern states during May and June, under warm, humid and unsettled weather conditions, but they can appear anywhere at anytime.

In the event of a tornado warning, immediately seek inside shelter in a cellar or a reinforced concrete building. Stay away from windows, but try to leave some open to equalize the pressure inside and outside the building. In open country you must quickly move away from the tornado's path at a right angle, or lie flat in the nearest depression or ravine. If you've got the time, dig a foxhole to get you below the surface, away from the wind.

Hurricanes are coastal storms that occur most often from June through October. They receive their energy from the warm waters of the tropical oceans. A tropical storm is considered a hurricane when the winds reach speeds of seventy-five miles per hour, but they can go as high as two hundred or more miles per hour. Although hurricane winds do much damage, the greatest cause of death and destruction is from flooding and drowning.

If your area receives a hurricane warning, stay inside wherever you are. If the building is on high ground, stay there until the storm is over. If not, leave low-lying areas, which are likely to be swamped by high tides. Secure outdoor objects. Board up your windows and doors.

In any kind of a severe storm like this the most important objective for the outdoorsman is shelter. The best advice, frankly, is to get back to "civilization" before the storm hits. But if you're stuck outside, hole into a cave or build yourself a shelter away from bodies of water that might flood and trees that might fall.

10

First Aid

This subject is a dangerous one. There has been disseminated a good deal of misinformation, and a good deal of correct instruction has been misunderstood or misapplied. What I'm going to do is to reprint here pertinent portions of a Guide that I used during my forty years of Government service: the U. S. Forest Service First Aid Manual, together with illustrations and addenda from various sources.

The following 6 steps shall be taken with seriously injured persons:

1. Examine victims thoroughly.
2. Treat, in this order, immediately:
   SERIOUS BLEEDING.
   STOPPAGE OF BREATH.
   POISONING.
   SHOCK. Keep victim lying down.
3. If at all possible, in cases of serious injury try to get help. Alert hospital if necessary.
4. Give nothing to eat or drink to an unconscious or internally injured person.
5. Make victim comfortable. Don't let him see injury. Be calm, cheerful.
6. Move only when absolutely necessary. Use prearranged plan and approved methods.

Wound Treatment

Any wound, no matter how small, should be touched only with a sterile pad or the best substitute, such as a clean folded handkerchief, sterilized with a match, boiling water, or alcohol. Don't breathe on wounds.

1. If possible, wash or somehow clean hands thoroughly before treating any wound.
2. Never touch wound with hand, clothing, or any unclean material.
3. Wash wound with soap, then do not touch it.

SERIOUS BLEEDING

CUT ARTERY OR VEIN

Symptoms
1. Cut artery: bright red blood spurts or wells up.
2. Cut vein: dark red blood flows steadily or oozes.

First Aid
1. Remove or cut clothing from wound.
2. *Always apply pressure at once.* Seconds count. In extreme cases loss of 2 pints of blood can be fatal.
   a. Apply direct, firm, strong pressure preferably on sterile dressing over wound first. Direct pressure on the wound will almost always control bleeding if enough pressure is used.
   b. If this fails to stop flow, apply firm strong pressure to nearest pressure point. See sketches on next page.
   c. If this fails, and the bleeding is life threatening:
      (1) Apply tourniquet (TNT) close to wound but with unbroken skin between TNT and wound.

Apply direct, firm, strong pressure.

Pressure points. Arrows indicate those most effective.

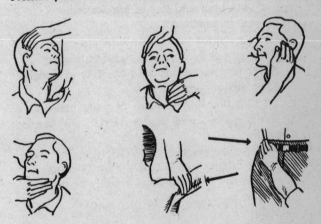

Applying a tourniquet, start to finish.

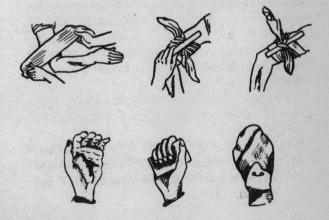

      (2) Apply TNT tightly enough to stop bleeding.

      (3) Do not release TNT, no matter how long in place, except by a doctor.

      (4) Use triangular bandage, towel, belt or flat material about 2 inches wide, wrapped around limb twice, then knotted.

      (5) Attach note to victim, giving TNT location and hour and day of application.

3. Additional instructions:

  a. Elevate injured part unless broken.

  b. Bandage tightly over sterile pad on wound.

  c. Never give stimulants until bleeding is stopped.

  d. Keep victim quiet.

  e. To stop bleeding in palm of hand place sterile pad in palm, close fingers over it, and bandage tightly.

  f. Also see information on WOUNDS.

INTERNAL BLEEDING

Symptoms

1. Restlessness
2. Anxiety
3. Thirst
4. Pale face
5. Weak, rapid pulse
6. Weakness

First Aid

1. Keep victim flat on back. Exception: If he cannot breathe due to lung puncture, prop up only slightly.
2. Turn his head to side for vomiting.
3. Keep him quiet, reassured.
4. Move him only in lying position.

NOSE BLEED

1. Victim sits with head thrown back, breathing through mouth, clothing at neck loosened.
2. If bleeding from one nostril only, press this nostril to middle partition for 5 minutes.
3. Apply cold, wet cloths to nose.
4. If possible, pack sterile gauze back into nostril.

STOPPAGE OF BREATH

SMOKE, GASES, DROWNING

Symptoms
1. Unconscious
2. Breathing stopped
3. Face and lips blue, flushed or pale
4. Pulse weak or absent; beat erratic

First Aid: Artificial Respiration by Back Pressure–Arm Lift (Holger-Nielsen) Method
1. Place victim face down, head lower than feet, loosen clothing.
2. Bend his elbows and place his hands one on top of other.
3. Turn face to side, chin up, cheek upon hands.
4. Check mouth to be sure air passage is not blocked.
5. Kneel on one or both knees at side of victim's head, facing him; place heels of hands just below line between arm pits, thumb tips touching, fingers downward and outward.
6. Rock forward on straight elbows, with steady pressure on back.
7. Rock backward, sliding hands to victim's arms, just above elbows, grasp arms, continuing to rock backward.

8. Raise arms until tension is felt, then lower arms. This completes the cycle, which should be repeated 12 times a minute for several hours, if necessary, or until doctor arrives.
9. Treat for shock.
10. Keep victim lying down, quiet and warm for 24 hours.

B. *Mouth-to-Mouth Resuscitation*

1. Clear the air passage.
2. Lift up under neck (extend chin) and pinch the nostrils together.
3. Inhale deeply. Seal your lips around victim's mouth to shut off loss of air. Blow air forcibly into victim's open mouth, maintaining regular rhythm of inhaling/exhaling.
4. Remove mouth, listen for return flow of air.

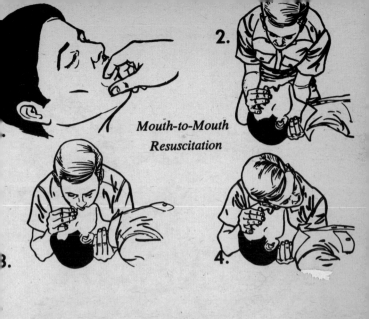

2.

Mouth-to-Mouth Resuscitation

3.

4.

C. Back Pressure (Shafer) Method

1. Clear air passage.
2. Position victim properly.
3. Rock forward, press down on hands.
4. Sit back, allow chest to expand.

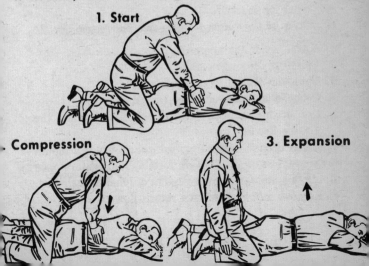

1. Start

Compression

3. Expansion

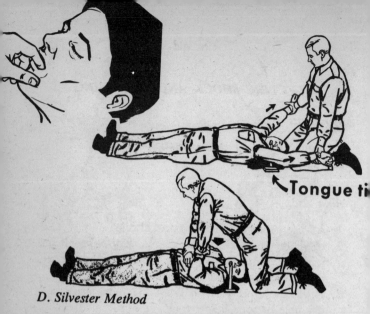

Tongue ti

D. Silvester Method

1. Clear air passage (Hold tongue forward).
2. Position victim properly (Place pad or rolled coat under shoulders).
3. Draw arms upward and outward.
4. Bend and cross arms over chest, press down.

E. Changing Operators (Holger-Nielsen Method)

1. Kneel beside the operator.
2. Match rhythm of operator.
3. Wait until end of a complete cycle.
4. Swing into place, continue operations at same rate.

ELECTRIC SHOCK AND LIGHTNING

Symptoms

Same as for smoke above, except there may be burns, and body may be rigid at first.

First Aid

1. Always protect yourself against shock.
2. If victim is on pole and rescue may take several minutes, compress his chest 12 times a minute, while rescue tackle is being adjusted.
3. If victim is on wire on ground, remove wire with dry pole or rope before touching him.
4. Apply Back Pressure–Arm Lift Method as above, then treat burns.

CHOKING

1. Hold victim upside down or bend forward as far as possible, then give sharp slap on back.
2. If breathing stops, apply Back Pressure Arm Lift Method as above.

POISONING

Symptoms

1. Pain in stomach and vomiting; diarrhea with food poisoning.
2. Flushed or bloated face.
3. Mouth may be burned.
4. Convulsions
5. Unconsciousness.

POISONS NOT ACID OR ALKALI

1. DILUTE: Give large amounts of fluid, 4 to 7 glasses of solution of 1 teaspoon of either baking soda or salt in 1 glass of warm water, warm dish water—or milk if caustics like lye or ammonia have been taken.
2. WASH OUT: *Induce* vomiting by tickling throat.
3. Give antidote, if one is known.
4. Give heaping tablespoon of Epsom Salts in water.

ACIDS

1. *Avoid* vomiting if possible.
2. Neutralize with alkali such as baking soda, magnesia, chalk, in water.
3. Give milk, olive oil, or egg white.

ALKALIES

1. *Avoid* vomiting if possible.
2. Neutralize with weak acid such as lemon juice or vinegar.
3. Give milk.

FOOD POISONING

Symptoms

1. Uncomfortable feeling in upper abdomen.
2. Pain and cramps.
3. Nausea and vomiting.
4. Diarrhea.
5. Prostration.
6. Unconsciousness in severe cases.

First Aid

1. Call doctor.
2. Never give a physic unless ordered by doctor.
3. Dilute and wash out same as for poisons not acid or alkali.
4. Keep victim warm, in bed.
5. If vomiting persists, give small drinks from glass of water containing teaspoon of soda.
6. Give him black coffee or strong tea.

SNAKE BITE

Prevention

1. Wear high shoes.
2. Watch for snakes.
3. Carry snake-bite kit.

Symptoms

1. Immediate pain.
2. Swelling, purple color.
3. 1 or 2 fang puncture points.
4. Weakness, short breath.
5. Rapid, weak pulse.
6. Vomiting, faintness.

First Aid: Remember Constriction, Incision, Suction

1. Victim must remain absolutely quiet.
2. Tie a band around limb, above bite and above swelling to restrict poison spread. Handkerchief, soft belt, a shoelace will do. Loosen it a little if limb gets cold or numb. Remove band for a minute every 15 minutes.

3. Sterilize knife over flame, then make ¼-inch cross-cut incisions through each fang mark.
4. Apply suction to incisions until doctor arrives. If you don't have a suction pump, suck out blood and venom, then spit it out, unless open sores are in mouth. Continue for 30 minutes.
5. When swelling spreads about 3 inches above bite, move band above swelling if necessary, make more incisions there, then apply suction.
6. Treat for shock.
7. Give plenty of drinking water.
8. If struck by snake when you are alone, apply band, cuts, suction if possible. If not, stroke down toward fang marks and squeeze out blood and venom. Then walk slowly toward help.

NOTE: A promising method for poisonous bites is called the L-C Treatment. However, in most survival situations the necessary materials are not available.

1. A tourniquet is placed directly above the bite.
2. The bitten area is placed in a pail containing half-sized ice cubes, or ethyl chloride is sprayed on the wound area. (This chemical should be applied only by a doctor.) Continue for about 6 hours.
3. The tourniquet is removed not more than 10 minutes after the ice treatment starts, and left off.
4. An incision is made only when a very large snake bites.

INSECT STING

1. Remove sting.
2. Apply paste of baking soda and cold cream.
3. Cold applications will relieve pain.
4. Calamine lotion will relieve itching.

BLACK WIDOW SPIDER, SCORPION BITES

Symptoms

1. Slight swelling, redness, tiny red spots.
2. Immediate burning, spreading pain.
3. Hard abdomen.
4. Fever, sweating, nausea.

First Aid

1. Keep victim lying down, quiet and warm. If he must be moved, use a stretcher.
2. Give deep hot tub bath to relieve cramps.
3. Get doctor immediately.

BEE STINGS

1. Do not try to pull out stingers. Pinching the venom sac will inject additional venom.
2. Scrape out sacs with a knife or other thin object.
3. Put ice on the sting as soon as possible. Application of household-type ammonia is almost always helpful.

NOTE: Hypersensitive persons or those sensitized by previous stings may have fatal reactions unless promptly treated medically. Inform any medical man of your bee sting history.

POISON OAK-IVY-SUMAC

Prevention

1. Wash body and clothing thoroughly with thick soap suds (yellow laundry soap best) in hottest possible water, then alcohol.
2. Avoid smoke from burning plants.

Symptoms

1. Skin red, swollen.
2. Small blisters, which may later enlarge.
3: Violent itching.

First Aid

1. Wash as above under PREVENTION.
2. Make paste by heating soap and water to consistency of lard, apply thickly to rash, allow it to dry, and leave on overnight.
3. Or use calamine solution.
4. Consult doctor about injecting extracts of poison ivy or oak to produce resistance.

SHOCK

Shock is a depressed state of all body functions caused by injury. Unless treated, the condition often results in death, although the injury itself would not be fatal. *Treat for shock in any injury case.*

Factors Contributing to Shock

1. Exposure.
2. Pain.
3. Rough handling.
4. Improper transportation.
5. Loss of blood.
6. Fatigue.
7. Broken bones and internal injuries.

Symptoms

1. Symptoms usually develop gradually and may not be noticeable at first.
2. Skin pale, cold, moist, clammy.
3. Eyes vacant, lackluster, pupils dilated.
4. Breathing shallow, irregular air hunger.
5. Nausea, faintness, or even unconsciousness.
6. Pulse weak, irregular, rapid, or even absent.

First Aid

1. *Position:* Keep victim lying flat. Raise legs 12 to 18 inches, unless head is injured or chest is punctured.
2. *Heat:* Keep victim only warm enough to prevent shivering. Save body heat by blanket underneath.
3. *Fluids:* Give a cup of warm water, milk, tea, or coffee, unless victim is nauseated or unconscious, injured, or an operation is expected.
4. Additional instructions:
   a. Keep victim quiet and undisturbed.
   b. If he is in intense pain inject 100 milligrams of demerol, if available, according to directions on packet. Otherwise, give 1 or 2 five-grain aspirin tablets with water every 4 hours.
   c. If injury is extremely serious, notify doctor that plasma may be needed.

BURNS AND SCALDS

Symptoms and Classification

1. First degree, skin reddened.
2. Second degree, skin blistered.
3. Third degree, skin cooked or charred, may extend to underlying tissue.

First Aid

For small first and second degree burns covering up to 1 percent of body surface (size of hand):

1. Place sterile gauze over burned area.
2. Bandage entire area snugly.
3. Rebandage only after 3 days.
4. For moderate sunburn, use vaseline.

For large burns of any degree:

1. If doctor or hospital is available within an hour:
   a. Treat for shock.
   b. Rush to hospital, untreated.
2. If in isolated area:
   a. Remove clothing from burn, cut around where it sticks, for doctor to remove later.
   b. Cover burn with cool, moist sterile dressing.
   c. Cover this with 8 to 10 layers of loose sterile or clean dressing.
   d. Dress burn so it cannot touch burned or unburned skin.
   e. Bandage snugly so there is moderate pressure on burn.
   f. Treat for shock.
   g. Control pain by hypodermic injection of 100 milligrams of demerol, if available, according to directions on packet.

(1) If pain persists, repeat in 45 minutes, then every 2 hours.

(2) Do not use demerol for skull fractures, or in case of illness.

h. If victim is conscious, he should drink all he can of solution ½ teaspoon baking soda or 1 teaspoon salt to 1 quart water.

i. Plasma is very important in early treatment of burns, so notify doctor that it may be needed.

j. DO NOT

(1) Touch burn with fingers.

(2) Breathe on burn.

(3) Apply antiseptic.

(4) Break or drain blisters.

(5) Change dressing. Doctor should.

NOTE: Large amounts of salty fluids leak through burns. They must be put back into the body or the person's life is in danger. Victim may drink up to 10 quarts of salt and soda in water, guided by his thirst. REMEMBER. SHOCK IS THE GREAT KILLER IN BURNS.

EXCESSIVE HEAT

The following illnesses can be prevented by taking salt tablets frequently:

SUNSTROKE

Symptoms

1. Headache.
2. Dizziness.
3. Red face.
4. Hot, dry skin.
5. Strong, rapid pulse.
6. Very high temperature.
7. Usually unconscious.

First Aid

1. Put victim in shade, lying on back, with head and shoulders raised, clothing removed.
2. Apply cold to head.
3. Cool body by wrapping in sheet and pour cold water on a small portion at a time; or use cold cloth, or cold cloths and ice bags.
4. Rub limbs toward heart through sheet.
5. Give cool drinks, no stimulants.

HEAT EXHAUSTION

Symptoms

1. Pale face.
2. Dizziness.
3. Vomiting.
4. Profuse sweating.
5. Moist cool skin.
6. Weak pulse.
7. Low temperature.
8. Fainting but seldom unconscious for long.

First Aid

1. Lie down, keep head level or low.
2. Drink solution of ½ teaspoon salt in ⅓ glass of water until 1 tablespoon salt is consumed in 6 drinks.
3. Give coffee or tea.
4. Apply external heat in severe cases.
5. Remove victim to circulating air.

SWIMMING CRAMPS

Symptoms

Cramps in the fingers, toes, arms, or legs are a common hazard in swimming. They are of little danger unless they cause panic. Such cramping is often caused by fatigue and overexertion.

First Aid

Relief is gained by stretching the muscles, or by simply changing your swimming stroke and relaxing. Rub or knead the cramped muscles. Float as much as possible to relieve strain.

INJURIES DUE TO COLD

FROSTBITE

Symptoms
1. Considerable pain in hands and feet, but not in cheeks, ears, nose.
2. Grayish white color on frozen tissues.

First Aid
1. Until victim can be brought indoors, cover part with woolen cloth or warm skin of victim or first aider.
2. Bring into warm room, but avoid direct heat.
3. Give him warm coffee.
4. Thaw out frozen part gradually in warm room, or in lukewarm water 72–78° F. (Cold water faucet is usually this temperature.)
5. Gentle massage near, but not on, frosted part with coarse dry towel, starting near body and working to tip to restore circulation.
6. When frostbite or frozen part begins to peel, like sunburn, any bland lanolin-base ointment will alleviate most discomfort.
7. Frozen tissue will swell, crack and blister, resembling frostbite or burns. WARNING: Do not treat with ointment.
8. Be careful that there are no contrictions anywhere to slow blood circulation!

PROLONGED EXPOSURE TO COLD

Symptoms

1. Victim becomes numb, drowsy.
2. He staggers, eyesight fails, becomes unconscious.

First Aid

1. Place him in warm room and apply Back Pressure-Arm Lift Method if breathing has stopped.
2. When victim reacts, raise room temperature slowly.
3. Give him hot coffee and put him in warm bed.

SNOWBLINDNESS

Prevention

Wear dark glasses in snow country, particularly in early spring and at high elevations.

Symptoms

1. Burning, smarting, sandy feeling in eyes.
2. Pain in eyes or forehead.
3. Sensitivity to light, eyes watering.

First Aid

1. Cold compresses on eyes.
2. Wash eyes with boric acid solution.
3. Mineral oil in eyes.

BONE FRACTURES

FRACTURE OF ARM OR LEG

Symptoms of Simple Fracture

1. Victim may hear or feel bone snap, and grating.
2. Pain and tenderness at break.
3. Inability to use injured part or to move adjacent joints.
4. Broken part may be swollen, deformed, discolored.

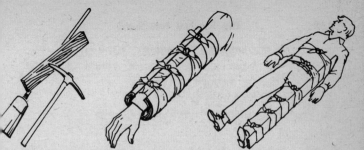

Left: *implements that can serve as improvised splints.*
Center: *newspapers can be used to wrap a fractured arm.*
Right: *a simple but effective leg splint.*

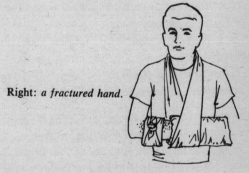

Right: *a fractured hand.*

Left: *a fracture of the toe.* Right: *handling a fracture or dislocation of the leg or ankle. Place pad around knee and ankle.*

Symptoms of Compound Fracture

1. Same as above, plus presence of wound extending from fracture through the skin.
2. Fractured bone may protrude.
3. Frequently there is severe bleeding.

First Aid

1. If doctor is nearby, do not move. Keep broken ends and adjacent parts quiet.
2. If bleeding, cut away clothing and control flow by sterile compress, then bandage. Use tourniquet (TNT) only as last resort.
3. If necessary to move, have splints, pads, and ties ready, then:
   a. Give complete immobilization to fractured bone and next joint in either direction from fracture, by well-padded splints.
   b. If the long leg bones are broken and victim must be moved some distance to doctor, apply traction splint, unless bone is protruding, in which case immobilize leg by placing sterile dressing over wound and splinting in place.
4. After splint is in place, examine every 20 minutes to be sure swelling has not cut circulation.

SKULL FRACTURE AND CONCUSSION

Symptoms

1. Bump or cut on head.
2. Victim dazed, unconscious.
3. Bleeding from ears, mouth, nose.
4. Pulse rapid and weak.
5. Pupils of eyes unequal in size.

First Aid

1. Keep victim lying down, warm.
   a. If face normal color or flushed, raise head and shoulders.

b. If face is pale, lower head slightly.
2. Move only if necessary, and then horizontally.
3. Give no stimulants.
4. Apply sterile gauze and bandage to open scalp wound.
5. If strangling from blood and mucus, lower head and turn to drain.

RIB FRACTURE

Symptoms

1. Severe pain on deep breathing or coughing.
2. Break may be felt by fingers on rib.
3. Shallow breathing.
4. If lung punctured, frothy, bright red blood may be coughed up.

First Aid

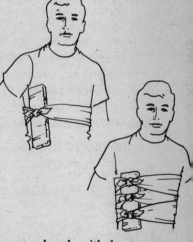

Objective is to control pain and restrict rib motion.
1. If lung is punctured, or rib is broken, do not bandage. Have victim lie quietly; move him lying down to doctor.
2. Apply 2 or 3 triangular cravat bandages around body.
   a. Tie first one loosely over break with knot over a pad, on side opposite break. As victim exhales, tighten knot.
   b. Repeat above with 2 more cravats, one above, one below, first one.

LOWER JAW FRACTURE

1. Place palm of hand below jaw and raise it gently to bring teeth together.
2. Support jaw with bandage under chin, tied on top of head.
3. If victim vomits, release bandage, support jaw with hand, and rebandage.

COLLARBONE FRACTURE

Symptoms

1. Fracture can sometimes be felt by finger.
2. Injured shoulder lower.
3. Victim usually cannot raise arm above shoulder.

First Aid

1. Put arm in triangular bandage sling, with hand raised above elbow level and ends of fingers uncovered.
2. Tie arm snugly to side of body.

HAND OR WRIST FRACTURE OR CRUSHING

1. Apply padded splint to front of hand, from middle of forearm to beyond fingertips.
2. Place arm in triangular bandage sling, palm down, with hand 4 inches higher than elbow.

KNEECAP FRACTURE

1. Straighten limb.
2. Tie limb to well-padded 4-inch board reaching from buttock to heel, leaving kneecap exposed. In emergency a pillow or blanket can be used instead of board.

DISLOCATIONS

Symptoms

1. Intense pain.
2. Deformity.
3. Swelling.
4. Loss of movement.

First Aid

1. Apply cold compresses.
2. If necessary to move victim, support dislocated elbow or shoulder in loose sling; if hip dislocated, place pillow under knees.
3. Keep other dislocations immobilized in dislocated position, except first two finger joints or jaw.

SPRAINS

Sprains are tears of ligaments supporting a joint.

Symptoms

1. Pain at joint.
2. Swelling.
3. Discoloring.

First Aid

1. Elevate the part, if practical, by putting wrist in sling, ankle on pillows.
2. Apply cold applications in early stage up to 6 or 8 hours; hot applications later.
3. If 1 and 2 cannot be done, immobilize part as much as possible by bandaging. Keep injured part quiet.

STRAINS

Symptoms

Pain in muscles, increasing stiffness.

First Aid

1. Rest injured muscle.
2. Apply heat, but don't blister.
3. Gentle rubbing upward on injured part.
4. Massage to loosen up muscles.

WOUNDS AND BANDAGING

All wounds, no matter how small, should be treated to prevent infection. When bleeding is not severe, infection is the chief danger. Unclean first aid is more dangerous than no treatment at all, except in case of serious bleeding.

First Aid

1. In isolated areas, if possible thoroughly wash wound with soap and water, then cover with sterile pad and bandage, otherwise cover and bandage until washing can be done later.
2. If wound is large enough so that it will have to be sewed up:
   a. After washing, cover with sterile gauze, then bandage and take victim to doctor.
   b. If doctor cannot be reached for several hours, after washing, close wound by finger pressure and apply butterfly taping, then bandage.
3. Small wound dressings need not be changed for several days, unless infected.

Bandaging

1. Always apply sterile gauze pad directly on wound, then bandage over this.
2. Never use absorbent cotton or adhesive tape directly on a wound, except a narrow bridge of adhesive sterilized over flame, to hold wound edges together.
3. Use a square knot and tie where easy to reach.
4. Bandage snug but not tight; ends of fingers and toes uncovered, if possible, to check on constriction.

PUNCTURE WOUNDS

1. Encourage bleeding by mild pressure.
2. Apply sterile pad and bandage.

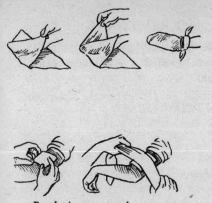

Bandaging a wound.

EYE WOUNDS

Object imbedded in eye or surrounding tissues:
1. Apply sterile pad and bandage, loosely if eyeball is injured; firmly otherwise.
2. Get to doctor.

To remove object not imbedded in eye:
1. Pull down lower lid to see if object is there.
2. If so, remove it gently with handkerchief corner.
3. If not, grasp upper eyelashes, have victim look upward, and pull upper eyelid forward and downward over lower eyelid.
4. Flush out eye with ½ teaspoon of boric acid in glass of water.
5. If object still there, put mineral oil in eye.

BLISTERS

1. Wash with soap and warm water.
2. Sterilize needle over open flame.

3. Puncture blister at edge.
4. Gently press out water or blood with sterile pad.
5. Apply sterile bandaid or dressing.
6. If blister has broken, wash dry with sterile gauze, apply sterile bandaid.

INFECTED WOUNDS

Symptoms

1. Throbbing pain, heat.
2. Much swelling, redness.
3. Pus and red streaks.
4. Tenderness, fever.

First Aid

1. Rest.
2. Hot applications of 3 heaping tablespoons of salt in 1 quart of water, preferably by putting infected part directly in the solution.
3. Change often enough to keep hot and continue for an hour.
4. Elevate part, then repeat hot application in 3 or 4 hours.

HERNIA

Prevention

1. Get firm footing and handholds when lifting.
2. Lift with your leg muscles, not your back—keep back straight.
3. Don't twist when you lift.
4. Get help with heavy loads.
5. Avoid heavy lifting and straining.

Symptoms

1. Swelling in groin appears suddenly.
2. Swelling may disappear when victim lies on back.
3. Pain is often disabling.

First Aid
1. Lay victim on back.
2. If hernia does not go back into place, lay him on stomach and bring his knees up under chest.
3. Lay on back again and apply compresses to hernia, whether or not it went back into place.
4. Move him lying on back to doctor.

INTERNAL INJURIES

Symptoms
1. Nature and extent of injury usually is not clear.
2. Severe shock is often present.

First Aid
1. Get a doctor.
2. Keep victim lying down, treat for shock.
3. Do not give him liquids or food.
4. Transport him carefully in a lying position.

BOILS AND PIMPLES

1. Do not squeeze.
2. Treat as an infected wound, with hot salt applications to draw to head.
3. Wipe off discharge with sterile gauze; apply sterile pad and bandage.

EARACHE

1. Do not allow victim to blow nose hard.
2. Apply hot water bottle to ear.
3. Drop in warm mineral oil.
4. If this not effective, try cold pads.

TOOTHACHE

1. If no cavities are visible, apply heat or cold to outside of jaw.
2. If there is cavity in tooth, clean out with cotton on end of toothpick.
3. Dip another piece of cotton in oil of cloves and insert in cavity.

TRANSPORTING VICTIMS

Do not be hurried into moving an injured or ill person. Poor methods can result in increased injuries. Victims often must be moved long distances under difficult conditions, so plan and execute the job carefully to avoid aggravating injury or shock.

Preparation

1. Always give essential first aid before transporting; then there is not so great a hurry to move.
2. Make victim as comfortable as possible; loosen tight clothing, and always treat for shock.
3. To put blanket under victim, pleat ⅔ of it beside him, grasp him at hips and shoulders, roll him about ⅛ turn away from blanket. Push the pleated part under him, roll him back over the blanket and ⅛ turn in other direction. Then pull blanket on through.
4. Be sure fracture cases are well padded.
5. If a compound fracture case has to be carried a long distance, traction splints on legs will help to decrease serious shock and make victim more comfortable. Watch for dangers of dislocation with too much traction. Traction is not used on arms except in rare cases where serious shock is expected.

6. Improvised stretchers are satisfactory for short distances, but for longer travel, especially through rough country, use the best equipment and manpower available.
   a. Folding type canvas or metal cots, or even chairs in some cases, are good emergency stretchers.
   b. An air mattress provides for greater comfort on a stretcher and therefore less shock danger.

Loading

1. To load or unload a stretcher, 3 bearers are needed, and a fourth is desirable.
2. Place stretcher close to victim, who is on back with feet tied.
3. Three bearers face victim's uninjured side, one at shoulder, one at hips, one at feet.
4. Bearers kneel on knees nearest victim's feet, place arms under victim, at neck, shoulder, back, thighs, legs, feet.
5. Bearer in command says "lift," all lifting victim together up on their knees. Bearer in command pushes stretcher against bearers' toes.
6. At his command, "lower," the bearers gently lower victim to stretcher.
7. Unloading procedure is reversed.

Carrying

1. To carry stretcher, bearers are on ends, and usually two on each side if terrain permits.
   a. Stretcher is raised and started off on given signals.
   b. The front and side bearers start on left foot, rear bearer starts on right foot.
   c. Victim is carried feet first except when carrying up hills, steep grades or stairs.

    d. Leg fracture victims are carried uphill feet first and downhill head first.

2. Watch victim for increased signs of shock, and apply shock treatment; and check his dressings.

3. Victim is usually transported with head lower than body, unless head is injured or if breathing is difficult.

4. Victim should be able to see where he is going.

5. Serious cases should be transported lying down.

6. Be particularly careful with head injury cases. Victim with injury to back of head should be laid on his side.

7. Never jackknife an injured person into the back seat of a car.

THREE-MAN LIFT AND CARRY. *At first command, "Prepare to lift," first man positions hands under patient's ankles and knees; second man positions hands under thighs and small of back; third man positions hands under shoulders and neck. At second command, "Lift patient," bearers slowly lift, supporting patient on their knees. At third command, "Prepare to rise," bearers turn patient slowly to his side until he rests against their chests. At fourth command, "Rise with patient," bearers slowly stand up.*

11

Mountaineering

Mountain travel techniques are based generally on experience, which in turn is acquired only through actual physical performance. However, experience can be replaced somewhat by the intelligent application of practices learned through study and careful observation. For example, travel routes may be established by observing the direction of a bird's flight in the morning or toward evening as it heads for water, the way trees grow or even the shape of snow banks. Bearings read from a compass, or the sun or stars can implement these observations and confirm original headings.

An experienced mountaineer carefully observes and surveys the surrounding terrain for the safest and most direct route that will get him out of his predicament or to his intended destination. A distant blur may be mist, dirt or smoke; a faint, winding line on a far-off ridge may be a man-made road or an animal trail. A blur in the lowlands may be a herd of cattle. You should plan your travel each day only after carefully reconnoitering the terrain. Study distant landmarks for characteristics that you can recognize from other angles and locations as you move along. Before you leave your emergency bivouac, study your back trail carefully. Do this often as you travel ahead. You may have to backtrack in order to take a new route. Again, after you pass, game may move out from cover to watch your movements, affording you an opportunity to acquire much-needed food.

Rain, fog or snow may hide the sun, and at times you may have to orient a course by observing landmarks such as vegetation, sand contours or snowdrifts that are effected by prevailing winds. Moving under such conditions is difficult until you can see streams, hills or a coastal area running in a definite direction.

Tips for the Mountain Traveler

Common sense will aid you in your trek through the vast high country wilderness areas, where nature has carved majestic peaks and canyons. The basic rules for mountain travel are:

> Know your terrain.
> Do not travel alone.
> Travel only in daylight.
> Keep together.
> Leave a route plan and schedule with family or
> friends.

Choose your companions carefully. The mental and physical strength of your party will determine what and where you can travel. Travel only as fast as the slowest member. Travel slowly and steadily, with short, frequent rest stops.

Study route and location often.

Allow plenty of time. Remember, you are out for pleasure. Don't make a hard job of it. You will want to

Climbing in the Wasatch National Forest near Salt Lake City, Utah.

enjoy the scenery along the trail and be able to return home rested and relaxed, not all worn out. Many outstanding and spectacular views are never seen by weary travelers.

If you are the leader or in charge of a party of hikers or mountain climbers, you are responsible for the well-being of the group and their safety, for the routes taken and equipment needed. Plan the jaunt at home with the other members of the party by studying the contour maps of the region you plan to enter. Study Chapter Two. Be sure that you are familiar with all trails, escape routes (in case of a forest fire, avalanche or sudden storm), and problems you are likely to encounter. Then decide on your party and route schedule.

Leave a trip schedule. It is important to leave a schedule with a responsible person as to your route, members in your party, equipment and your anticipated return time from the area, allowing extra time for normal problems. Include location and description of the vehicles used. Sign out with Park or Forest officials, if possible. Also inquire about local rules and conditions in your expected travel area. Some areas are closed to hikers due to hazardous fire conditions, others because of the danger of avalanches or for other safety reasons.

Horse Sense

Never pack into the mountains with saddle and pack stock unless you are experienced in handling, feeding, packing and caring for the animals in remote regions far from a veterinarian. If you do not have these skills and do not know how to shoe a horse, better take a packer or guide along. Always be careful near horses and mules so that you do not get kicked by them.

To save yourself from a bad fall or the chance of

an animal slipping and falling on you, dismount and walk in rough terrain. Lead your saddle horse across or over dangerous spots in the trail.

Never trust your own or strange animals even though you may know their habits well. Someday they may leave you afoot far from the pack station or the home corral.

This mountain climber is descending, or rappelling off. Behind him is Anniversary Mountain in Victoria, B.C. Notice the double rope passed under his thigh, across his body, and over his shoulder.

Recommended Essentials for Mountain Travel

Lug-soled boots for firm footing and easy-on, easy-off clothes suitable for wind, rain or cold weather will help regulate your body temperature. Your pack or rucksack should be light in weight and large and strong enough to carry all necessary equipment and food for safe mountain travel. Take plenty of matches, a candle, extra food. You may be delayed a day or more due to weather conditions or an emergency. Take extra clothes, first aid kit, small trail survival kit (See Chapter Seventeen), compass, map, BSA pocket knife, flashlight and a lightweight plastic tarp or mountain tent for emergency overnight shelter. A warm sleeping bag is essential for your sleeping comfort.

Have the proper gear for the terrain you plan to climb or cross. Rock, snow and ice require special technical equipment and experience, and you should know how to use the gear correctly.

Hard hats for all members, pitons, climbing ropes, sunglasses, sun and windburn lotion, pulleys, carabiners, ice axes, slings, marking route wands, insulation and a warm down sleeping bag may be needed.

A long-range weather report is also important to your safety.

Glaciered Peaks or Rock Cliffs

This type of terrain requires technical skill and will give harsh treatment to those not well trained, not properly equipped or not in excellent physical condition. Many outdoor hiking and climbing clubs conduct special classes where you can acquire training and experience in these facets of mountaineering.

Acquire further training or take along a qualified guide before attempting this type of sport. Safe high mountain travel and climbing rest on the shoulders of all who enter or visit the wilderness areas. Spectacular scenery from these high points will pay for your energy in climbing them. And you will have the satisfaction of special achievement later.

Be Alert to Certain Dangers

There are numerous places on the North American continent where mountain ranges can be negotiated on foot in a single day by following a glacial route.

Nevertheless, always be alert to unexpected dangers such as avalanches loosened by a warming sun, or caused by members of your own party, and rocks set in motion by erosion.

- Don't clown, throw or roll rocks. It's dangerous!
- Use great caution near crevasses! Dangers on glaciers will be mostly hidden. Deep crevasses (cracks in the snow and ice) are often hidden with a layer of snow or bridged by delicate snow bridges.
- Even the sun will be a hazard. It will weaken the snow bridges, burn your skin and blind your eyes if you do not take special precautions.
- Probe the snow bridges.
- Use face and lip lotion.
- Wear snow goggles.

Steep snow slopes can and do avalanche—even those with only a 20 percent slope. Cornices can break off, too! The edges of easy-to-walk snowfields will melt back considerably and warrant your special attention and caution. Without special skills and equipment, ice and snow slopes can be extremely hazardous. Hikers can make unexpected slips or slides called glissading. If you lose control when glissading, you can end up in a pile of rocks or drop over a cliff. If you should ever lose control when glissading, dig the point of your ice axe into the ice to slow you down or stop you in time to avoid an accident.

Anticipate High Country Problems

Never underestimate high country terrain or the weather.

Your own fatigue can be a problem. It can lower your body resistance, fog the mind and weaken your judgment, as well as weaken your legs.

Travel uphill slowly but steadily. Conserve energy as you will be far from immediate help in case of trouble.

Never enter wilderness country if you have a head or chest cold. It can turn into something serious in the cold backcountry!

Turning Back

Don't be ashamed of turning back or aborting your trek before reaching your objective. It may take some of the pleasure out of your mountain jaunt, but it could save your life.

Don't take a chance by splitting up or dividing the party by sending an ill member down the mountain with another member. All members of the group should return at once unless you have an exceptionally large party. Too many mishaps can occur when a hiking group is split.

You must anticipate the strength of your companions

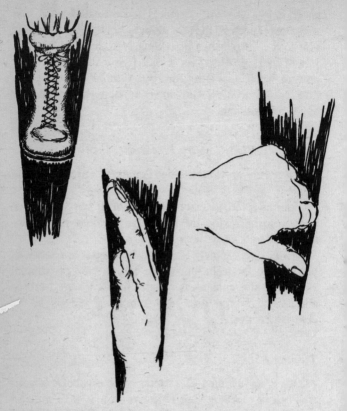

Above and on facing page are proper hand- and foot-holds for good climbing technique.

for the return trip. Weather could add to its complexity. FOG obscures your landmarks. RAIN makes every descent treacherous. WIND will steal your body heat. THUNDER and LIGHTNING will warrant a hasty retreat from all high points and ridges. Stay away from single trees, too!

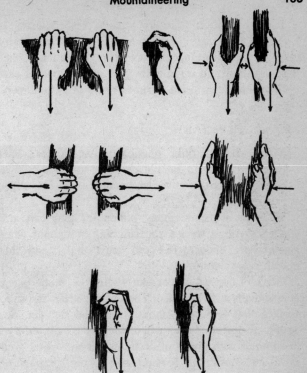

Descent Problems

On the descent, when you are tired, hungry and per-haps wet or cold, your group will tend to separate and take shortcuts in the rush to return to the road head. *Keep together!*

When descending, foot- and handholds below you will be difficult to find. Your boots will have to search out firm holds on uneven terrain, slippery grass or pine needles. Downhill travel over loose gravel or stones can turn an ankle, dislocate a knee and blister your feet if you are not watchful.

Some mountain travelers attempt fast descents by sliding down steep snowfields. Play it safe. Always check the slide distance on foot before glissading. Otherwise you may end up in a crevasse or as a basket case!

Snow can turn to ice in shady spots or at sundown.

Ice and Glacier Travel

Many glaciers offer possible travel routes. Their main contribution to emergency travel is that they serve as avenues across or over mountain ranges into different watersheds.

To cope with the many difficulties that can arise when traveling over ice and climbing mountains where glaciers are encountered you must understand their makeup and nature.

Glaciers consist of two parts: first, a valley glacier is essentially a river of ice. The lower glacier has an ice surface that is bare of snow during the summer. Secondly, an upper glacier where the ice is covered even in summer with layers of accumulated snow that grade down into glacier ice. Ice and snow slopes, although not part of the glacier proper, generally are found adjacent to glaciers, and usually are of similar composition.

Ice and snow slopes are immobile since they are anchored to the underlying rock slopes and terrain. A large crevasse will separate such terrain from the glacier proper and define the boundary between the active and anchored ice.

Crevasses

Whenever you find glaciers you will run into the crevasse problem. Ice is plastic near its surface, but not sufficiently so to prevent cracking as it moves forward and downward over the irregularities in its bed.

Park Rangers at Mt. Rainier National Park rescue a man from a crevasse.

Crevasses and ice fractures in a glacier surface that will vary in width and depth from only a hair-width to many feet. Crevasses normally form at right angles to the direction of greatest tension, and since within a limited area tension usually is in the same direction, crevasses in any given area tend to be roughly parallel to each other. Crevasses generally develop across a slope, so when traveling up the middle of a glacier, you will nearly always encounter transverse (crossing at right angles to the main direction of the glacier) crevasses.

Very similar to the movement of a river, the ice moves more slowly near the margins or edges of a glacier, than it does in "midstream." Even the gentlest slopes may contain crevasses.

All bridges across crevasses should be tested before attempting to cross them.

On glacial ice, crevasses may show up as white streaks of snow bridges between the bluer ice of the shelf or glacier, or there may be *no sign whatsoever* on the surface of a dangerous bridged crevasse.

Snow Bridges

On snowfields bridges may show as regular, dish-shaped depressions running for distances in near straight lines. Stay away from areas showing numerous surface cracks or snow domes, for where there is considerable glacial movement, there are bound to be many danger-ously bridged crevasses.

Old slumped bridges may be stronger than flatter bridges of newer snow. Probing these bridges with an ice axe or ski stock is safe only for most man-hauling or dog team travel. Crossing with heavy equipment means heavier probes are necessary *proving* snow bridges are safe.

Traveling Plateaus

Long dish valleys are safest, with the greatest danger of crevassing near the crests of north facing slopes. Ex-posed rocks are usually best approached from the west-ern or lee side where drifting usually bridges any danger.

Snow drifts or waves of six inches to six feet in height may be crossed at a flat oblique angle, never at right angles. These snow crests indicate the direction of the prevailing winds, and may serve as a clue to direction in an emergency.

Snow domes formed by blizzards may be in any direction, depending on the direction of the prevailing high winds of the blizzard. Don't depend on these domes for direction!

Remember that ice cliffs, whether glacial, shelf or otherwise, are extremely dangerous. Not only can you fall from the top of or through a bridged crevasse, but, also, you could be buried by ice falls if you are walking near the base. On warm days the whole face of a cliff or shelf may fall without warning. This is no place to chip ice to melt for drinking water. Don't take chances.

These mountain climbers are too close to the edge of that crevasse for safety's sake.

Travel on Moraines

Where the snout of the glacier has pushed forward as far as it can go—that is, to the point at which the rate of its melting equals the speed of advance of the ice mass—a terminal or end moraine of loose rocks is usually found. The moraine may be formed by the ice and rock debris pushed forward or it may be formed by a combination of this and other processes.

When glaciers are much crevassed, moraines may be the only practical routes of travel. Ease of movement or progress along moraines depends on the stability of the debris that composes them. If the material consists of small rocks, pebbles and earth, the moraine usually is loose and unstable and the crest may break away at each footstep. If larger blocks of ice and rocks encompass the moraine, they usually have settled into a compact mass and progress over them may be safer and easier.

When you travel on moraines, it is best either to proceed along their crest or, in the case of lateral moraines, to follow the trough which separates it from the mountain side. Since the slopes of moraines are unstable, there is great risk of fall and injury. See the illustration here.

Medial moraines are much easier to travel than lateral ones. However, do not rely on them as routes of travel for long distances since they may peter out

Terminal, lateral, and medial glacial moraines can be seen in this view of the 4,000-foot wall of Luna Creek Cirque in Mt. Baker National Forest, Washington.

and disappear beneath the glacier's surface. Only rarely is it necessary for a party traveling along or across moraines to be roped together.

Crossing Rivers and Streams

Due to variations in the amounts of water released by the sun's heat, all glacial rivers and streams fluctuate. The peak of the flood water usually occurs in the afternoon as a result of the noonday heat of the sun on the ice. For some time after the peak has passed, rivers draining glaciers may be unfordable or even unnavigable; however, by midnight or the following morning, the water may recede so that fording is both safe and easy. When following on foot a glacial river that is broken up into many shifting channels, choose routes next to the bank rather than getting caught between two dangerous channels.

Glaciers that discharge torrents of water are called "flooding glaciers." There are two basic causes of such glaciers: namely, the violent release of water carried on its surface as a lake, or the violent release of large lakes that have been dammed up in tributary glaciers due to blocking of the tributary valley by the main glacier. This release is caused by a crevasse or break in the moving glacial dam coming opposite the lake, which then roars down in an all-enveloping flood. Witness the several towns in the Alps that have been literally wiped off the map in the past years, due to these glacier lakes breaking loose.

Normally these flooding glaciers can be recognized from above by the flood-swept character of the lower valleys—the influence of such glaciers is sometimes felt for many miles below. Hunters, explorers, mountain climbers and prospectors have lost their lives while rafting or crossing otherwise safe rivers because of a sudden flood disgorged by a side tributary and descending in a roaring white wall of water, taking everything before it.

Fording Streams

Every outdoorsman traveling on foot or with pack outfits through wilderness must ford some streams. These may range from small, ankle-deep streams that

Roped-up party crossing an ice field in the Rockies.

rush down from side canyon walls and valleys to large snow- or ice-fed rivers. The latter are so swift that you can hear boulders on the bottom being ground together by the current. If these streams are glacier-fed, follow the advice detailed above and, before attempting to ford such streams, allow them to decrease in strength during the night.

First, you must find a ford that is safe to cross. Be sure to find a high spot that commands the river below you and examine the valley below. Level stretches where the river breaks into several channels are best.

Watch for timber growths, since they indicate where the channel is deepest.

Look for obstacles that might hinder getting up onto the opposite bank, especially if you must cross with saddle and pack animals. Large ledges of rocks which cross the stream often indicate the presence of rapids or canyons below.

When choosing a crossing, whenever possible follow a course that leads across the current at about a 45-degree angle downstream.

Never attempt to ford a stream directly above or even close to a deep channel or rapid waterfall.

Choose a place where, should you lose your footing, you will wash up on a shallow bank or sand or gravel bar below the ford.

Try to avoid rocky places, if possible, for a fall can cause serious injury. However, an occasional rock that breaks the current may be of some assistance to you.

Depth is not necessarily a deterrent if you can keep your footing. Some deep water runs more quietly and more slowly and may be safer than fast shallow water. You can always dry out your clothing later. There may be spots that are easier to swim across than to wade.

Before entering the water be sure to plan exactly

what you are going to do and how you are going to do it.

It is a good idea to remove your pants and under-drawers and lash them on top of your pack with your firearms and binoculars. The water will have less grip on your bare legs. Keep your shoes and socks on to protect your feet and ankles from rocks and to give you firmer footing. Shift your pack well up on your shoulders and have the straps so that you can release the pack instantly in case you are accidentally swept off your feet. You will probably find your pack and gear on a sand or gravel bar downstream.

Poling

A strong pole will aid you in crossing. Use the pole on the upstream side where the current tends to push you down on the pole and lift your feet from under you. Plant the pole firmly on the upstream side and firmly plant your feet with each step. Lift the pole a little ahead of you and downstream from its original position but still upstream from you. Step below the pole each time. Keep the pole well slanted so that the force of the current keeps the pole against your shoulder.

Only experience can enable you to judge water and the swiftness of its flow, but remember that there is always danger when fording.

Take all possible precautions.

Be sure that all harness and lead ropes are tied up so that the animals cannot become tangled. The animals will pick out their own route and will swim when neces-sary once they enter the water.

Burros are the most difficult to get to enter water and sometimes you are forced to lead them across yourself.

A heavy pack on your back is to your advantage, so

don't worry about it. Just remember to have the straps adjusted so that you can slip out of the outfit quickly if necessary. Nothing helps you keep your feet better than weight. I have often added rocks to my pack when crossing rather swift streams like the Hoh, Sol Duc and others on the Olympic Peninsula and those in Alaska.

Mountain Rescue Procedure

Everyone entering a mountain wilderness should know what action to take if a member of the party becomes seriously ill or is injured or killed.

- Size up the situation quickly!
- Render first aid to the injured as soon as possible.
- Stop and think over the whole situation. Remain as calm as you possibly can, then get command of all the facts so that you will have the proper information for the authorities when you reach a phone, or, if you send a messenger, he will have the pertinent facts.
- *If* victim is dead, protect the body from the elements if possible. If you can handle the situation with your party and get any injured to the nearest medical aid, fine! However, in the case of fatalities, *don't* ever remove a dead body without the permission of the County Coroner!
- If outside assistance is required, make a list of:

  (1) Number of persons injured.
  (2) Extent of the injuries so far as you can ascertain.
  (3) Exact location of accident.
  (4) Time of accident.
  (5) Manpower, rations or food and equipment at scene.

(6) Name and address (phone number if possible) of victim.

(7) Names and addresses of other members of party and any witnesses.

(8) Notify the County Coroner if there are any fatalities, and find out if he wants the body removed.

- Send for help. If help is needed, send two messengers out *if possible*. In case one of the messengers sprains an ankle, the other can continue to get help. Always leave one person with the victim.
- Mark your route on the way out. Hurry, but be careful, so you reach aid.
- If you can reach a telephone, the following are the agencies that will give you the most help: (1) District Ranger of park or National Forest you are in; (2) Mountain Rescue Organization of state accident occurred in; (3) Sheriff's Office of county accident is in; (4) State Highway Patrol or State Police or Troopers. Give *them* the information listed above, and the following:

(1) Distance by road and trail, and approximate distance off trail; (2) If scene can be reached by helicopter; (3) Type of terrain and approximate time it will take rescuers to reach scene of accident; (4) Equipment, rations and approximate manpower required. (Special equipment such as shovels and probes needed in cases of avalanche); (5) Where you are phoning from, and where you will meet the rescue party. Stay at the phone until assured by responsible authorities that experienced assistance is on the way! Wait for rescue party and guide them in if possible. Be sure to follow your back trail so that the rescue party doesn't go astray. On reaching the scene, lay out signal panels,

or be sure that radio schedules are made on time with Air-Sea units, Civil Air Patrol, helicopters or private aircraft assisting in the rescue mission.

- Take no chances while bringing out victim.
- After the rescue, when the rescued have been attended to, don't forget to thank those that helped—thank the rescue teams.
- Hold a board of review inquiry at your next club meeting on how and why the accident occurred, and what could be done to prevent an accident of this type in the future.

12

Cold Weather Survival

Modern man needs a basic knowledge of cold weather survival techniques if he expects to camp, hunt or explore in the frigid mountain recreational areas of the United States and Canada. Cold, not food or water, is the most critical factor in these areas. A person stranded in terrain of this type must know how to supplement the protection given by any clothing he may be wearing when he finds himself in difficulty. It is imperative that he salvage everything from his boat, plane or motor vehicle that will help him to survive until rescue units can reach him. It may be weeks after an accident before a survivor can be located, since inclement weather—strong winds, fog, snow, heavy rain or a "white-out" (icy fog)—may keep search aircraft grounded and ground crews under cover.

The problems facing a survivor in any of the cold regions of the world are of the greatest magnitude. Temperatures recorded in our states like Montana, Wyoming, Colorado and parts of the Dakotas indicate that they experience colder weather than normally found

A Portland mountain climbing club making their way up the hogsback toward the 11,245-foot summit of Mt. Hood, Oregon.

in may parts of the Arctic. In the East blizzards have reached nearly 250 miles per hour!

A trek into the winter wonderland can be an inspiring and exhilarating experience. The air can be clean and pure and the woods and mountains beautiful. Nevertheless, a sudden storm can occur with unexpected fury. Great snow banners and icy plumes start to flare from the high rocky peaks and ridge tops. The sky darkens, snow starts to streak past and, suddenly, visibility and known objects are blotted out. Visibility is almost zero; a white-out occurs. A day's outing can turn into a survival situation.

It has been thought by many that man cannot survive in the extreme cold of the Arctic and the colder regions of the northern tier of states, yet the Eskimo has been able to clothe and feed himself and survive in the frozen regions of the Arctic throughout the years. It is just a simple matter of knowing how.

Not long ago, while on a vacation fishing jaunt in Alaska, William Waters became lost for 67 days, living on wild berries, plants and whatever he could scrounge off the land. He finally made his way to a river where he hailed a boat coming downstream and managed to locate the old tote road where he had left his car over two months before.

How to Use Snow as an Insulator

Rangers and snow surveyors have learned to conquer the problems of cold weather survival. So can you.

However, because he has been living in a controlled environment, the average outdoorsman has lost his ability to survive in snow without special equipment or knowledge in making snow work for him in times of emergency. Wild animals understand the insulating quality of snow, and the warmth it has when used as an insulator. Wild creatures use snow as a friend while some men panic when they are lost in snow country.

In other words, snow itself can be a positive asset rather than a deterrent to survival. When a person accepts this premise, his chances of survival are much greater.

Several years ago, Lt. David Steeves of the Air Force survived nearly two months in the high mountains of Kings Canyon National Park when his aircraft exploded. He injured both ankles parachuting into a basin near the 14,000-foot level, where he spent two weeks without food until his ankles had healed enough to enable him to work his way down to the 9,000-foot level at Simpson Meadows, where he found a small trail crew cabin. He later killed a deer with his pistol. As the snow receded, he was able to make his way over Granite Pass, where a pack outfit found him and took him on into Cedar Grove.

Many of you no doubt have read or heard of the ordeal of Helen Klaben and pilot Ralph Flores, who survived in subarctic Alaska in 1963 when they had to make a forced landing. It was 42 days before rescuers located them. You can survive if you get into a cold-weather situation of this sort if you will go prepared and use common sense.

Good Health a Must

What the Rangers and Royal Canadian Mounted Police are beginning to be concerned about is the older individual—40 years and up—who travels alone. He's usually soft and often physically unfit for meeting emergencies in high-country winter conditions. Chances of survival in an emergency under cold weather conditions depend on fast, carefully planned operations. Extremely low temperatures accelerate the action of shock, even with minor injuries.

In planning a long safari over snow, the first point to consider is general physical health of all members of the party. No one should go if he has a heart condition, lung problems or any other serious limiting physical impairment. Regardless of the type of vehicle used there is always the possibility of a breakdown. Each member should be physically able to walk out on skis or snowshoes if necessary.

Snowmobile Travel

Winter vehicles that skim across snowy, high-altitude terrain faster than a mountain goat in summertime pose new problems for rangers in the mountainous national parks and forests. The increasing use of the gasoline-powered, lightweight vehicles, operating on runners and power tracks, places a new responsibility on the rangers for the safety of forest visitors. Almost 100,000 snowmobiles were sold in one year, and their popularity is increasing. Trappers, prospectors and explorers are penetrating the far north with these gas-powered vehicles. Many Eskimos are now using skimobiles instead of dog teams.

One safety factor in skiing, snowshoeing and snowmobile travel is for several persons and vehicles to travel together. For safety, no travel should be undertaken during heavy snowstorms. Another dangerous period is in the presence of high wind and extremely low temperatures—ideal conditions for avalanches to run.

Winter sportsmen are cautioned not to go together across possible slide areas. They should proceed one

Most snowmobile accidents happen at night. The commonest cause is breaking through ice. Collisions with cars are also a major cause of incidents.

at a time with at least one of the party in a position of safety to observe.

If caught in severe weather, skimobilers and other travelers should stop their machines frequently to warm up the riders with a few minutes of vigorous exercise. Rangers recommend the "buddy system" for checking each other's faces for telltale dead white spots of frost-bite.

Cold and Wind

We have all heard the expression, "chilled to the bone." Many outdoorsmen are not aware of this danger-ous weather phenomenon that can appear suddenly, generally from late October to the middle of March. This atmospheric condition is known to weathermen as the "chill factor," a term used to identify a condi-tion that results when low temperature and high wind are combined. The usual effect is always a lower tem-perature than the thermometer indicates. So beware, it can kill you if you are caught far from shelter!

In spite of warm clothing the peril exists for thou-sands who participate in outdoor winter activities in our recreation areas. Persons exposed to a moderate chill factor situation may experience only extreme dis-comfort. As temperatures drop and winds increase, the problem can turn critical in a very few minutes.

How to Check

Before you set out for a day of winter sports activi-ties, check with your local weather bureau or Coast Guard station and find out what wind conditions may be expected for the day. If you are able to predict the potential hazards of the wind-chill factor, you may

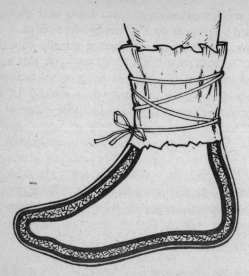

Emergency footwear for cold weather. To keep your feet as warm as possible use an inner sock, then stuff padding—dry grass, feathers, stuffing from a snowmobile or aircraft—to cushion the inner sock and the outer sock. Then wrap your parachute, tarp or other fabric around your foot and tie it above your ankle.

avoid becoming another winter victim. If you are already in the field and the temperature continues to drop —watch out for any increase in wind.

Protective Clothing

What really determines the kind and how much clothing you should use is the wind-chill factor. Thermal insulated or wool long-john underwear, wool shirt, and windproof pants and parka or an eiderdown jacket plus warm socks and water-resistant boots and gloves are standard battle gear on wet, windy winter days.

If you feel that you are dressed warmly enough for say 40°F., but soon begin to shiver—you just are not dressed appropriately for the day's wind-chill factor, which may lower the temperature to actually 16°F.

Temperature by itself is an unreliable gauge of comfort. It indicates only how cold the air is, not how cold it feels. And wind speed alone isn't much help in making decisions about dress. But combine temperature and wind speed, as weathermen and rangers do, into a wind-chill factor, and you have a reliable guide for clothing yourself against the bitter bite of winter.

What Wind-Chill Is

Wind-chill factor is a measure of how rapidly the body loses heat under certain wind and temperature conditions. For example, at zero degrees with no wind, you do not lose body heat as rapidly as when the temperature has climbed up to 20°F., but the wind is blowing a very brisk 18 miles per hour, making an actual temperature of approximately −12°F.

On a warm mild winter day, dress accordingly, but carry extra warm clothing along in a knapsack in case the weather changes later in the day accompanied with wind. If your clothing becomes damp from perspiration or from sleet or rain—wind chill can kill quickly—so hunt shelter and warm up at once!

Determining Wind-Chill Temperatures

The United States Weather Bureau will furnish up-to-date weather information, and hourly forecasts are available any time of the day or night. Make a note of the predicted winds and temperatures, and then apply these figures to the Wind-chill Chart shown here. This chart was developed for use by Park and Forest Rangers who patrol the winter scene.

The chart is simple to use. First locate the existing (or predicted) temperature on top of the horizontal line. This will indicate local Fahrenheit (F) temperature. Next, find the existing (or predicted) wind velocity in the vertical column on the far left under the heading Wind Speed (m.p.h.). Now follow the line of figures down from Local Temperature and across from Wind Speed. The equivalent temperature is at the point where the two lines intersect. For example, a reading of −4°F. on the top horizontal line and a wind speed of 25 m.p.h. on the left vertical line—gives an equivalent temperature of −50°F!

Another point you must remember is that when you are moving through the air as you do when sailing an iceboat, skiing or operating a snowmobile you should always figure in your approximate speed which will add another cold-chill factor to the above figures.

Snow surveyors and others who travel or patrol the winter backcountry heed the winter cold-chill factors to avoid cold weather sickness, injuries or death. So can the winter sportsman!

NOTE. A free wind-chill chart may be obtained from the Information Office, Bombardier, Ltd., Decarie Blvd., Montreal, Quebec, Canada. Included is information on how to dress properly to withstand winter cold.

Panic and Exhaustion Are the Real Dangers!

Many cases of death due to exhaustion and exposure have been attributed to the victim freezing. A person

WIND SPEED	LOCAL TEMPERATURE (F)										
	32	23	14	5	-4	-13	-22	-31	-40	-49	-58
5	29	20	10	1	-9	-18	-28	-37	-47	-56	-65
10	18	7	-4	-15	-26	-37	-48	-59	-70	-81	-92
15	13	-1	-13	-25	-37	-49	-61	-73	-85	-97	-109
20	7	-6	-19	-32	-44	-57	-70	-83	-96	-109	-121
25	3	-10	-24	-37	-50	-64	-77	-90	-104	-117	-130
30	1	-13	-27	-41	-54	-68	-82	-97	-109	-123	-137
35	-1	-15	-29	-43	-57	-71	-85	-99	-113	-127	-142
40	-3	-17	-31	-45	-59	-74	-87	-102	-116	-131	-145
45	-3	-18	-32	-46	-61	-75	-89	-104	-118	-132	-147
50	-4	-18	-33	-47	-62	-76	-91	-105	-120	-134	-148

For Properly Clothed Little Considerable   Very Great Danger
Persons   Danger   Danger

DANGER FROM FREEZING OF EXPOSED FLESH

Wind Chill Chart

lost in the wilds wearing normal winter clothing should
bore down into a snowdrift, sheltering his hands underneath his armpits, with his knees pulled up under his
chin. This way he can survive the night. If he has a map
or other papers, he should protect his chest by button-
ing the paper inside his jacket or parka for further insulation. Naturally he will spend a very cold night, but
he won't freeze to death in the temperatures in most
areas. His chances of survival, however, would be almost nil had he exhausted his energy in a futile, terror-
stricken attempt to get out of the snow to find a warmer
place to spend the night.

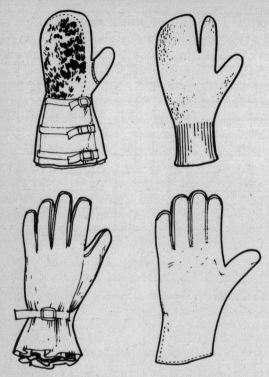

Types of gloves and mittens.

Cold and freezing are obvious dangers. But in studying the circumstances involved during my many years experience in cold weather survival, one thing becomes clear. The real dangers are not cold, nor freezing, nor the snow itself. They are panic and exhaustion.

A few years ago in southern Idaho nine sportsmen lost their lives during a snowstorm—not by freezing but by exposure and exhaustion. The temperature during this particular storm did not fall below 28°F. Two men of the group crossed several mountain ridges and found a cabin and there, in what should have been relative safety, died from exposure and sheer exhaustion. All the men in the group were wearing adequate, warm clothing and, if they had traveled slowly so as not to perspire, had remained calm and merely sought shelter from the wind when night set in, they could have survived the night.

Cases like this are too numerous to record here.

Human beings involved in snow survival situations must replace fear of the cold with respect and understanding. Persons entering cold and snow terrain should have a knowledge of wilderness craftsmanship before they set out. See the Woodlore Chapter (9).

Minimum Equipment

The minimum equipment that should be taken on any trip over snow should include:

> sunglasses
> matches in a waterproof container
> candle
> warm sleeping bag
> proper clothing
> cross-country skis and poles and ski wax, or a pair of "bear paw" snowshoes. (Beware of the new plastic snowshoes: they can become brittle in freezing weather and crack or break.) Skis are excellent to travel on if the individual is skilled in their use.

A lightweight 9 x 12 plastic tarp can be a life-saver. It can be made into several types of shelter or used as a roof on top of skis when making a snow hut. See the Woodlore Chapter for further details on this tarp.

First Things First

No matter whether you are a lost hunter, or a survivor from a plane forced down in snow country, you will need shelter, warmth, food and water—in that order.

To survive for any length of time in cold weather, man must have a minimum of equipment so that he can build a shelter, a fire and a trap or snare for food animals. In other words, he must have wilderness know-how.

Hints That May Save Your Life

- Don't exert yourself or you will perspire and your clothes will become damp. You can freeze to death within a few hours.
- Conserve body heat by building the quickest shelter you can to keep out the cold wind.
- Get a fire going as quickly as you can. Don't build your warming-cooking-signaling fire under a tree limb where melting snow will drip on it!

Making a Survival Camp

The first decision to make if you become lost or stranded overnight is the best and safest site for your survival bivouac. You must not locate your shelter in a possible avalanche path. Generally, avalanches start from the top of a mountain, building up terrific speed and force as they move downward—sweeping everything before them until they dissipate their force over a wide level area. An avalanche path may be recognized as a steep, comparatively bare area or scar on the mountain slope having few or sheared-off trees.

A safe survival site is within the cover of large trees or on ridge tops since avalanches usually travel down gullies or draws. Avalanches have occurred with slopes of only 20 percent grades!

When you have picked a safe location, you must decide whether to construct a lean-to on top of the snow or whether it would be better to hollow out a snow cave. (See the chapter on Woodlore.) Ideally, the temperature should be around zero before a snow cave is attempted.

The Snow Cave

No matter how carefully you build a snow cave, at temperatures between 20°F. and zero, body heat will melt the roof of the cave, permitting moisture to drip down during the night.

If temperatures are ideal and you decide to build a snow cave, the direction of the prevailing wind must be taken into consideration. This is important because the mouth of the cave should be on as steep a slope as possible. This will be the lee side of the snow bank, away from the wind.

Ideally, the cave should be built in an almost vertical bank and can be hollowed out to leave a roof no thicker than two or three feet. Skis or snowshoes may be used to dig and hollow out the snow cave. In some types of snow an icy crust forms on the surface, but it is relatively easy to hollow out a cave once this has been cut through.

After the cave has been hollowed out, make a hole

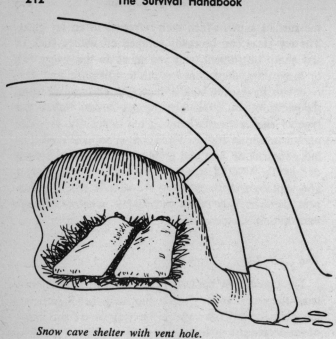

Snow cave shelter with vent hole.

from the interior of the cave to the outside of the snow pack. It can be poked through with a ski pole or limb. This is to be used as an air vent in case you light your candle.

Generally, snow contains enough air to supply adequate oxygen unless a small one-burner knapsack type stove is lighted. Then an air hole must be vented in the ceiling.

If you stay in a snow cave for several days, a glaze will form on the inner side of the cave. Body heat melts the surface snow, which then refreezes to an icy glaze. The icy glaze can be easily scraped off with a stick or any sharp instrument, and you must do this every two or three days, depending on the temperature.

If you have ever built a snow hut or cave in warm temperature, you know why it must be cold before this type of shelter can be constructed efficiently. At temperatures above 10° to 20°F., the snow will melt during construction and the builder will get wet. This is one of the WORST possible things that can happen in any winter survival situation! Repeat: in freezing temperatures you must avoid getting wet, whether through perspiration, condensation, dunking or whatever.

The Lean-To

The opening of the lean-to should always face away from the wind. If no wind is blowing, the direction of the prevailing winds can be ascertained by the shape of the snowdrifts. A long, sloping drift with a sharp drop on one end indicates that the wind is blowing toward the sharp drop.

The Wind-Shield Shelter

If the temperature is too high to make the construction of a snow cave practical, and if no boughs are available to build a lean-to, build a wind-shield shelter. This is simply a snow wall with an opening that faces away from the prevailing wind.

WARNING! Whether you decide to build a lean-to, a snow cave, wind-break or other type of survival shelter, one very important fact to remember is that it must be done at the proper pace—fast enough to keep warm, but not so fast that you perspire. Remember,

*At the top of the facing page is an arctic lean-to. Where
evergreens may be obtained, the shelter may be built on
two A-frames with bough-thatched roof and ends. Such
a frame may of course be covered with a parachute or
similar material. The chief virtue of a lean-to is shelter
from the prevailing wind. When the snow is 3 or more
feet deep with drifting, different types of shelter are
called for. At the bottom of the opposite page is an upright tree shelter. The lower branches may be chopped
off as the snow down to the roots is excavated. A small
fire gives some warmth. A felled tree shelter (above) is
made from a large evergreen tree that can be cut 5-7
feet above the ground. By tunneling snow and chopping
off bottom limbs, using them to thatch open spaces between limbs on top and side, a snug shelter may be built
under the hole.*

moisture is a real and deadly hazard. Wet clothing loses insulating quality quickly, and is almost impossible to dry in a survival bivouac camp.

Building a Fire

In cold-weather snow country starting a fire from scratch can be an ordeal. The prospect of building a fire without matches in snow or wet terrain is not a pleasant one. Moreover, having matches doesn't mean that you are going to be able to build a fire. You will need *dry* tinder, kindling, heavier fuel and a certain amount of skill. That means being prepared for emergencies where you might need to build a fire quickly. The experienced outdoorsman takes along various types of fire starters such as Heat-Tabs or fire-bars (small highly inflammable cubes), a metal match, waterproof matches, a cigarette lighter and sometimes a small 6-power magnifying glass (however, the latter can only be used under ideal conditions). In addition to the above list, I personally add a candle and a small can of lighter fluid, plus a few pieces of waxed paper. Rangers and seasoned mountaineers who patrol the winter back-of-beyond country adhere rather rigidly to the techniques outlined here.

1. Select a site on level ground sheltered from the wind and away from overhanging branches so that melting snow will not drown the fire. If in thick timber, it may be necessary to put some sort of shield high over the top of the fire to keep rain or melting snow from dripping off the limbs onto the fire.

2. Once the site has been selected, the snow should be removed down to bare ground or the fire should be placed on a log platform to keep it from sinking down

into the snow. The logs or tree limbs should be green and about four to six inches in diameter and from two to three feet long. In this manner you can construct a platform which will prevent your fire from melting its way into oblivion. One layer will do the trick, but two layers set criss-cross will do a better job.

3. All fire material should be ready and close at hand so that once the tinder is lighted, larger fuel can be added slowly until the fire is in full force.

Heat Reflector

Building some type of heat reflector makes more efficient use of your fire. The logs selected for this purpose should be somewhat longer than those used for the fire platform (depending on snow depth). Two logs are pushed into the snow or ground at a slight angle leaning toward the fire, but approximately twelve to eighteen inches away. Against these posts, aluminum foil can be stretched or small logs or canvas can be placed on the back of the upright post supports to help reflect the heat towards you or your shelter opening.

Sleeping Arrangements

Once the shelter has been constructed, and your fire started, your sleeping arrangement becomes most important.

All snow should be brushed from clothing and boots.

Your outer garments should be removed and put under the sleeping bag for insulation whether or not pine boughs are available. All other clothing and boots must go inside the sleeping bag for the night.

Many experienced winter travelers remove all clothing except heavy underwear. Part of the outer garments can be folded for a pillow.

Your boots should be placed beside your body where they can stay warm. If you leave your foot gear outside your sleeping bag, they will be frozen solid by morning. Frozen boots are not only difficult to put on, but are likely to freeze your feet or cause frostbite. It can take hours to thaw out frozen boots.

To keep boots pliant, they must be thawed out very slowly—not too close to a fire or the oil will dry out and the leather will become brittle. I learned the hard way in my younger, inexperienced days. Result: I lost both my large toenails!

To generate warmth and body heat within the sleeping bag, lie on your side and simulate riding a bicycle, moving hands and legs vigorously until all your extremities are warm.

Do not attempt to go to sleep until you are completely warm.

Your head should be covered, along with your neck and shoulders, but not your face. If your face is kept within the bag, frost will collect from your breath. Fluff up the sleeping bag before crawling into it for best insulation.

It isn't possible to freeze in your sleep. You will awaken as soon as you get cold just as you would if you were in your own bed at home. If you are awakened by the cold, go through the same exercise as indicated above, running in your sleeping bag. Open and close your fists and move your toes up and down or rub them with your hands until you are comfortably warm and have a good blood supply.

After the warming-up period, you should be able to

sleep one or more hours, depending on the temperature in the area.

You may have to go through the warming up exercise off and on all night, but you won't freeze to death.

The Next Day

When the night is over, you must make a decision while you are relatively warm in the sleeping bag as to what you will do the rest of the day. Generally, it is best to improve your temporary home and stay where you are. There will be men in aircraft, snowmobiles and other types of rescue vehicles looking for you.

If it comes to walking, skiing or snowshoeing out, decide which direction, and how far you think you can go, and what route you will take to get to your planned destination.

If you decide to travel, be sure to allow yourself sufficent time before dark to construct another survival shelter. Of course it is generally wiser to stay and improve the survival bivouac camp you already have constructed, thereby saving your energy and letting the search party come to you.

Survival on Sea Ice

Much of the information on cold weather survival also applies to sea ice survival. Your movements after crash landing, if this should be the case, should follow as closely as possible the check list given below.

- Take immediate care of any injured personnel.
- Check your clothing to make sure it provides maximum possible protection against cold and wet.

- Establish a temporary shelter immediately. If possible build a fire inside the shelter. Retaining body heat is your most immediate problem once you land on ice. Keep out of the wind as much as possible.
- Try to establish radio contact with rescuers if you have a workable set.
- Make a survey of the surrounding area to determine the safest camp site, considering the availability of food and water and the closeness to the wrecked boat or crashed aircraft if it is still remaining on the sea surface.
- Build the best wind-free camp you can.
- Try to find the nearest safe landing area for use of rescue aircraft and mark it. Check to make sure that the ice is thick and solid enough for rescue aircraft to land.

Building Your Arctic Shelter

On sea ice construct your shelter on solid ice floes as far away as possible from open water or from cracks that may open into water leads.

The only materials you will have available for shelter building are snow, ice, part of your aircraft or boat and parachutes. If you have a life raft it will make an excellent shelter with the canopy erected. Be sure to anchor the raft securely so that wind will not blow it over or away into open water.

Snow of a texture suitable for cutting into blocks for an "ice-house" or igloo will not be found on open ice but usually forms in the lee of pressure ridges or ice hummocks.

Level off a circular space ten feet in diameter. Build

a circular wall of snow or ice blocks at least four feet high. In the center of this circle build a pillar of snow blocks higher than the snow or ice block walls. Stretch one or more parachutes or the raft sail canopies over the wall and pillar, and drape excess material over outside walls for extra insulation. You can also make the walls square instead of circular and use a life raft for a roof. Chink all cracks with snow, but be sure to leave a small hole or opening for ventilation.

Dig snow from a trench around the outside border of the snow wall and tuck away excess canvas or parachute material into this trench and anchor it tightly by replacing the snow.

Cut an opening for a door 90° from the prevailing wind; and screen it with a tunnel or L-shaped entrance of snow blocks. This type of shelter is suitable for four or five persons. In the year and a half that I spent in the Arctic and subarctic, I found I could build a rectangular snow block house, 6 x 8 feet, in two hours. Eskimos can build a snow shelter in about 45 minutes if there are two or three in the hunting party.

If sleeping bags are placed on top of some type of insulation and two or three persons snuggle up closely, they can sleep more or less warmly. Having one or two candles lighted will help cut cold.

Food

Your only available food besides any rations you may have been able to salvage on polar ice are game and foods from the sea. Game animals include polar bear, seal, and occasional arctic foxes. Birds may be found in the summertime. They can be caught with baited fish hooks.

Snow trench made of ice blocks. Bottom: *Cutting snow blocks to build a survival shelter.*

The Decision to Stay or Travel

Unless you know that you are within walking distance of land, stay at the scene of the crash or wreck or as close to it as ice conditions will permit. Of course, if you are on ice that is breaking up, you will have to travel to the nearest stable ice or to land before you make your emergency camp.

Travel conditions on sea ice vary from place to place and from season to season. The smoothest ice is that frozen in protected fjords or bays; and the roughest, the pressure ridges formed between the fast ice to the shore and the moving pack.

When traveling the sea ice, be sure to carry your life raft for crossing open stretches of water. Don't risk a dunking or you will die of cold shock within 5 to 15 minutes!

EQUIPMENT FOR WINTER CAMPING: MY PERSONAL CHECK LIST

aneroid barometer (optional)—an aid to identifying elevation and keeping records

anti-fog stick to keep eyeglasses from fogging

balaklava wool helmet (optional)

bandannas (2), large size

belt or suspenders

camera and accessories

can opener, turn-twist type, leaves edges of can smooth, safer

compass, declination adjustable with sighting line

firearms and ammunition (optional, unless hunting)

first aid kit, small size, plus 12 codein-aspirin tablets, 12 sulfadiazene tablets, a mild laxative, and 2-inch roll of adhesive tape (sufficient for party of four)

flashlight and batteries, pen size, one each member

flashlight, head-lamp type, one per party

foil, aluminum, one roll

glasses, dark, extra pair, with case

handkerchief, white

hat with brim or billed cap with ear muffs

hot-water bag for sleeping bag comfort and storing water overnight

knapsack, Kelty Mountaineer Model or Bergan type

knife, BSA or utility type, with can opener, screw-driver, etc.

map, topographic, large-scale, of area to be traveled

matches, waterproofed, in waterproof container

mittens (2 pair) wool liners, ski cloth outers

moccasins or snowpacs to wear inside shelter

muffler or wool scarf

notebook and pencil

parka, close weave, water repellent, windproof, knee length, zipper front

poncho or ground cloth, can be used as roof in snow cave

sewing kit, small Army type (optional)

shirts (2), lightweight wool

ski boots

ski pants, windproof, water repellent, loose knees, smooth, tight weave with zippered pockets

ski wax, climbing and gliding

skis with bindings and poles

snowshoes, bear-paw type for climbing, Yukon type for cross-country (optional)

soap, small bar

socks (2 pair), lightweight wool inner; 2 pair heavy-weight outer socks half-size larger

sunburn lotion, zinc oxide or cream type

sweater, lightweight wool

tent, 2-man Army arctic 6 lbs. 6 oz., or Mountaineer Model 3 lbs. 4 oz.

Thermos bottle for hot drinks and storing water (optional)

toilet paper

towel and toilet articles

underwear (2 suits), wool, two-piece loose weave. Sleep in one pair while pair worn during day dries in sleeping bag. (New knitted or insulated type best.)

watch, water and shock-proof, wrist type

whisk broom for sweeping snow off clothes and out of tent

Don't forget to include in the first aid kit personal medicants needed. Fish hooks and line may be added if you wish.

All equipment should be packed in a good strong packsack so that it will be instantly available in emergency.

13

Surviving on Water

Disaster at sea!

You may think of a tremendous ocean liner dead in a raging sea, the huddled passengers on the tilting decks of a ship and, nearby, a glassy iceberg shines cold and blue in the moonlight.

Disaster at sea isn't your problem, you say. You aren't planning an ocean voyage, so why bother being overly dramatic when all you own is a 21-foot inboard with a 75 h.p. motor. Even though small-boat accidents seldom make headlines or the evening newscast, the U. S. Coast Guard has figures to indicate that they are a lot more likely to happen than most people think.

Sudden bad weather—a squall or heavy seas—can capsize your boat. You can hit a submerged rock in unfamiliar waters, or go aground on a sand reef created during a winter storm. An engine may explode and your boat will catch fire and burn.

Why Air-Sea Rescue Is Difficult

Survival at sea can be more rugged than being forced to survive in a desert; the ocean is a much vaster area of many millions of square miles, and the weather can be very mean. It is difficult to spot a small life raft or boat from a fast-moving search plane. Again, the sea may be so rough that it is impossible for the seaplane to land after sighting survivors. Water, food, radio, life raft and medical supplies must be dropped and surface craft sent for.

In the far northern regions, as well as in the Antarctic, fog and white-outs hamper surface vessels in locating survivors of sea or air tragedies.

How to Prevent Boating Hazards

Fire, explosion, collision, sinking, running aground, becoming lost or running out of fuel can be avoided by using common sense, by being prepared, and by obeying the Coast Guard regulations concerning small craft.

In many states the Coast Guard requires an annual inspection before they will give you a yearly sticker. They also board boats at will to make sure the running lights are in order, the proper number of life jackets are aboard, the bilge is clean and dry and that the engine is in good working order.

Even if you have only a five h.p. on an inflated rubber raft, follow the standard Coast Guard regulations. They are the rules of the road in the boating world.

In any event you should think out ahead of time the procedures necessary to deal with the more common emergencies you might encounter. Then, should a disaster occur, you will be prepared and your actions are more apt to be automatic, fast and probably correct.

It is just as important for the small-boat operator to hold fire, man-overboard and other boat drills as it is necessary for the captain of a large ship. Your life and those of your guests or family are just as precious as those of passengers and crew on board a commercial vessel. Also, it is wise to acquaint at least one person on your boat with the operation of your craft and its motors.

If you sail on a large body of water, make sure you have studied Chapters Two and Three in this book. They are about map reading. Substitute chart for map. The information on Orienting Yourself might be necessary if you should become lost in a fog or go off course during a storm.

And in the woodlore section there is information on knots and ropes that every sailor should have. In fact, you shouldn't take a canoe from a float without knowing the proper nautical hitches for tying it to a pier.

Your Safety Kit

All fishermen, yachtsmen, sailors and aircraft pilots should carry a sheath knife with a lanyard attached to their belts, a referee's whistle for signaling and a pair of leather gloves in their hip pocket to protect their hands if they are forced to slide down a rope or line from the deck of a vessel.

Also every boat should have on board a knapsack containing the following articles:

> waterproof flashlight
> blanket
> sweater
> shirt
> pair of socks
> small first aid kit
> sun glasses
> suntan lotion
> line and fish hooks
> hat

Man Overboard! An improper start from a dock throws the unwary occupant over the side. The operator made a jack-rabbit start without checking to see if the guests were properly positioned. A boat should be taken from a dock very slowly.

If you have these and any other items you might need for your particular locale in your kit bag, it may save your own life and other lives as well.

Stopping

For safety reasons and good seamanship, every boat owner should know his boat's braking or stopping distance. To do this, locate an area clear of boat travel. Find a buoy, pile or fixed marker and drive your craft past it at full speed. The instant it passes the marker, cut the throttle. Observe the distance required for the craft to come to a stop. Generally, the moment it drops off plane it will begin to slow rapidly.

You can stop very quickly with an inboard by closing the throttle quickly, putting the clutch in neutral, and shifting quickly to reverse and opening the throttle quickly. However, you must let the motor or engine idle a moment in neutral to save the clutch from shearing apart. By using the above guide, you should be able to decide quickly whether you have room to stop or should turn quickly when an emergency situation suddenly confronts you.

Man Overboard

This emergency occurs more often than one realizes. Here's what you should do.

Immediately swing the stern away from the victim. This will reduce the danger of the propellers striking the person in the water.

Even if the person can swim, throw a life preserver ring to him. Don't aim at the person in the water. You might hit and injure him, causing him to drown. Toss it upstream so he can grab it as it moves toward him.

Don't hesitate to use any lifesaving device close at hand: buoyant seat cushion, wooden grating or

anything that will assist in keeping the person
afloat. Speed is essential!

Keep the person in view. If it is night, direct your
light on the person in the water.

If possible, maneuver to approach the victim downwind, or head into the sea. Of course, the manner
of approach depends on good judgment based on
existing conditions at the time: whether you are
alone in the boat, have maneuvering room, and
the availability of other assistance.

If you have someone who can help in the boat with
you, have him don a life preserver with a line attached to the boat, and go over the side to help
the person who fell overboard.

Getting on Board Again

It is often difficult to climb into a boat from the water.
If the victim is weak, cold or injured, he may not be
able to climb aboard by himself without assistance.
In small boats, the weight of a person suspended from
the side might be enough to tip the boat so it ships
water and swamps. The proper procedure in boarding
small craft is to come over the stern or bow, depending
on the boat's size and construction. Obviously, one
should stop the propellers when bringing in a person
over the stern. In an outboard motorboat, where there
is danger of accidentally bumping the controls, the
motor should be turned off. If you have a swim or
boarding ladder, drop it over the side to assist the person aboard.

Fire Afloat!

Most marine fires are preventable. A skipper who
keeps his craft shipshape, has clean bilges and sees to

proper stowage of gear and inflammables may never face the problem of fighting a boat fire at sea or while docked. Greasy or painting rags should not be stored or thrown into a locker.

But despite a boatman's best efforts, fires do occur. Fire on the water can be a most terrifying experience. A person's surroundings are burning. He is faced with no place to retreat except into the water. In a sense he is trapped, unless he has a dinghy in tow or a rubber life raft on board. Few small recreational boats carry this kind of equipment. If swimming is the only alternative, don a life jacket or ring. If you are not a good swimmer, don't attempt to swim ashore even a short distance. Distances are deceiving. You might get a cramp and drown!

Fire-Fighting Equipment

A skipper of a "well-found" boat in shipshape condition will have his fire-fighting aids on board and stowed handily. On a small boat, fire gear is usually limited to one fire extinguisher and a bailer bucket or large can, depending on the size of the craft and state and Coast Guard regulations.

Fires are extinguished by one of two methods— namely cooling and smothering—or a combination of both. A fire requires heat as well as oxygen and fuel to support combustion. Remove one of these and the fire will go out. Extinguishing agents such as dry chemicals, carbon dioxide and foam smother and, to some extent, cool fire. They are most efficient on oil or grease fires when the extinguisher is directed at the base of the flames. Don't forget, water surrounds your boat—use it, but not on grease, oil or gasoline fires! Throw burning material overboard.

FIRE! The dread of all sailors. A Coast Guard boat tries to save a cabin cruiser which exploded during fueling at Edgewater Marina, Cleveland, three hours after delivery to its buyer. The three persons on board suffered first and second degree burns.

How to Maneuver When Afire

When underway, the forward motion of the boat will fan the flames and smoke aft. So stop, or reduce speed. If the fire is aft, head into the wind. If the fire is forward, put your stern to the wind. This will tend to prevent the flame and smoke from spreading to other sections of the craft, and will keep the flame and smoke away from you long enough to get your portable fire equipment into action.

Abandoning Your Boat

Remember, many small boats have floated for long periods after being in an accident. If you abandon your craft due to fire, explosion, swamping or capsizing, don't leave the area. Rescue searchers can spot your boat in the water more easily than they can see you swimming through the waves.

Other Emergencies

If you have hit something and a hole is forward on a planing hull, it is sometimes possible to make shore by simply maintaining planing speed. Otherwise, you will have to plug the hole with whatever is at hand, such as rags, stuffing from seat cushions, etc. If the hole can be reached from inside, it should be plugged with waste, jackets or whatever comes handy. Passengers can bail if necessary. Set your speed for the least leakage.

If you run aground, kill the motor immediately and check for hull damage. Check for fuel spillage, especially if you hit hard. Wipe up all spilled fuel immediately. Next, try to back off under power if the cooling intake isn't fouled. If power will not move you off, shift passengers and cargo aft and try poling off with an oar or boathook. If the shoal is shallow enough, go overboard and brace your back against the bow and push. Sometimes having a crew member or passenger run back and forth to rock the boat as you push will do the trick.

Tips on Abandoning Ship

- A damaged or partly swamped boat will be more or less buoyant and will keep you afloat. Most craft

Helicopter lifts man to safety while his mate clings to debris following a boating disaster.

have built-in buoyancy tanks or material to keep them afloat.

- Unless the boat is afire, stay with it. It will be easier for search craft to locate you.
- If there is time, give the proper distress signals: at night, red flares or rockets; smoke pots in daylight; radio distress calls—May Day May Day—SOS in international morse code, etc.
- Wait until the vessel comes to a complete stop; try to get away in a lifeboat or raft.
- If you are forced to go over the side on a line, fire hose, cargo net or ladder, be sure to put on your gloves. Go down hand-over-hand. Never slide down, or you will rope-burn your hands even with

gloves on. This can be very painful and your hands can become blistered and infected and further irritated by salt water and any fuel that may be on the water from leaks from the damaged ship.

- If there isn't time to lower a lifeboat or raft, go over the weather, or windward, side of a sinking vessel, otherwise the wind will drive a drifting ship down on you. If the sea is running high, leave the foundering boat by the bow or stern, whichever is lower in the water. If the propellers are still rotating, leave by the bow.

- If it becomes necessary to jump overboard, fold your arms tight across your life jacket. Then, selecting a clear area below, jump with your legs extended and feet together, and swim under water as far as you can. On surfacing, spring high and sweep your arms wide about you, thus pushing the flames away from you. Get a quick breath of air and swim under water until clear of any burning fuel.

- If you have a cork life ring or cork life jacket, throw it over first and jump after it. If you wear it when you jump, it may injure you or knock you out.

- If you are wearing a pneumatic rubber life jacket and can swim, jump in before you inflate it and swim a safe distance away from the vessel.

- If you are wearing a kapok life jacket, be sure all ties and drawstrings are drawn tight and tied securely before you jump.

- If you enter the water wearing an inflatable life jacket, discharge only one of the attached CO_2 cartridges. One will inflate your jacket enough to keep you afloat. Save the other until needed.

- Shoes are a great disadvantage if you are forced to swim without a life jacket, so get rid of them, even

though their lack can be painfully felt on boarding
a rescue vessel with steel decks that often become
so heated from the sun's rays that you cannot walk
on them in bare feet.

- Stay clear of a sinking vessel to prevent being
sucked under water when the vessel takes its last
plunge. Stay clear of any oil- or gas-saturated
waters, but stay in the vicinity until it sinks.

- Don't worry if fuel oil *does* get into your eyes. It
will inflame them for several days, but do no
damage. Wounds and injuries that have come into
contact with fuel oil heal normally.

- If you are in the water and your boat is drifting
rapidly away, don't tire yourself uselessly by making a futile attempt to swim and overtake it.

- Don't attempt to swim ashore without a life jacket
or other buoyant object—you might develop a
cramp or collapse from shock from an injury in-
curred in the accident. Nevertheless, if you know
how to relax in the water, you are in little danger
of drowning, especially in the ocean, where the
body is of lower density than sea water. If you
are an experienced swimmer and are able to float
on your back, you can rest yourself by treading
water.

Survival Swimming

Even if you can't swim, here is a method that will
keep you afloat for hours. You can even make a nearby
shore with a broken limb. It is called drown-proofing,
and this is the way it works:

STEP ONE. Inhale a deep breath and drop your head
forward in the water until your chin is on your chest.
Relax your whole body and let your hands dangle at

Survival float stroke, in sequence, repeated for as long as necessary.

Survival swim stroke, in sequence, repeated for as long as necessary.

your sides. If you tend to be plump and your hips start swinging upward, exhale a little air through your nose or mouth, and your body will return to a vertical position. Now rest, just hanging in the water vertically. You should now feel cold air on the back of your head, since a few inches of your head will protrude above the surface.

STEP TWO. After a few moments have elapsed, but before you need to breathe again, leisurely cross your arms in front of your head, with your forearms together, one knee toward your chest. Now extend your other foot behind you. Make your movements slowly, smoothly and easily, so that you remain in a vertical position, with your head lolling and relaxed.

STEP THREE. Raise your head swiftly but smoothly, stopping with your chin still in the water. As you raise your head, exhale through your nose, beginning while your face is still under water and continuing as it emerges.

STEP FOUR. When finished exhaling, inhale through your mouth. To keep your mouth above water while you inhale, gently sweep your palms outward and step downward on the water with both feet. If you move too vigorously, you will plunge your head and shoulders out of the water; you only need to raise enough so that your chin will be at water level.

Experiment to see how much oxygen you must have for each step.

STEP FIVE. Having inhaled, close your mouth and drop your head toward your knees. Remember to *relax*. Let yourself go limp as outlined in steps one and two. If you start to sink a foot or so below the surface, it is because you failed to drop your arms after putting your head in the water. When you need another breath, swing smoothly into steps one to five again. If your lungs and chest feel tight under water (mine usually do), you are resting too long or are not exhaling deeply enough.

The Swimming Stroke

Now that you know the technique of how to stay afloat for hours, but don't know how to swim, and you want to reach a nearby life raft or head for the shore in the distance, this is how it may be accomplished:

STEP ONE. After following steps one to five, take a deep breath. As your head submerges, push down gently with your hands (fingers together) so you won't sink too deep.

STEP TWO. Now tip your head forward to a face-down position. Bring your hands to your forehead and move your legs into a running position, with the rear foot raised as high as possible. This will tend to swing your body into a more-or-less horizontal position.

STEP THREE. Extend your arms forward and toward the surface with your hands together. The moment they are fully extended, make a frog-kick (like a frog kicks with its hind legs).

STEP FOUR. As your feet come together from the frog-kick, slowly sweep your arms forward, outward and then back in the breast stroke, in effect pulling yourself through the water, finishing the stroke with your hands at your sides. Slow and smooth action does it. Use just enough energy to keep yourself moving forward and to keep from sinking. The whole idea of the technique is to move slowly and gently so as to save your strength and energy. Generally you will move forward at about one mile per hour.

STEP FIVE. As you glide forward and upward, remember to keep your body relaxed and your hands at your thighs, and begin to exhale through your nose. Don't wait until you need a fresh breath, but begin returning to the vertical position by bowing your back, bringing both knees toward your chest and raising your hands toward your head, exhaling as your body rises.

STEP SIX. As your body continues toward the vertical, by extending one leg in front of you, bring the other knee up to it. Now cross your arms in front of your head, forearms together, palms out.

On the Life Raft

- When you swim over from a sinking ship and find a mass of survivors around a raft or in an overcrowded lifeboat, hang on the hand-line that encircles the gunwale. Don't try to climb aboard.

- Help get any injured persons and the women and children aboard. No matter how closely packed or uncomfortable you may be, try to help others by being calm, cheerful and quiet.

- Be sure that all injured persons have been given first aid if you are in charge of a boat or raft.

- Take seasickness pills as needed if you or some of the passengers have them.

- Half your ordeal is won once you get aboard a raft or lifeboat. Experience over the years has shown that of survivors adrift for more than 24 hours, half have reached shore or have been rescued within four or five days. Almost all lifeboats are spotted and picked up within two or three weeks.

- Search the area for any missing persons before leaving the area. Salvage floating equipment; stow and secure all items and check rafts for proper inflation, leaks and points of possible chafing.

- Bail out your lifeboat or raft if necessary. Be careful not to snag your raft with shoes or sharp objects. Remember that the bottom of the raft is very thin and that the water is very deep under it!

- If there is more than one raft, connect rafts with at least 25 feet of line. Connect rafts only at the lifeline around the outer periphery of the raft. Unless the sea is very rough, shorten the line if you hear or see an aircraft. Two or more rafts or lifeboats close together are easier to spot than scattered ones.

- If there is an emergency radio on board, put it into operation at once. The directions are on the equipment. After your first May Day transmissions, use the emergency transceiver only when aircraft or a ship is known to be in the area, to save the batteries as much as possible.

- As soon as possible, squeeze out all your wet clothing. Do not take off all your clothing unless the weather is warm and dry, and the wind moderate. Clothing protects you from sun and windburn. You can become sunburned even on a cloudy day. Undress and dry your garments layer by layer. Protect your head from cold and sun by keeping it covered.

- Be sure that you have washed off any gasoline or fuel oil you have on you.

- In cold oceans, put on your exposure suit if you have one. Keep bundled up and as warm as you can. Rig a wind-break, spray shield and overhead canopy if possible. If you are with others, huddle together for warmth. Exercise regularly.

- Protect yourself against cold winds, rain, spray and sun. You can rig a canvas screen or an awning with a boathook, oar, mast or whatever is at hand.

- Your feet should be kept dry and covered if possible. To prevent "trench foot," pay special attention to your feet. If you have on wet boots and socks, remove them as quickly as you can. If you have a pair of clean dry socks in your survival kit, now is the time to put them on.

- If your craft is wet and low in the water and waves continually sweep across it, keep your shoes on, but if you notice that your feet are beginning to swell, remove them.

- If you remove your shoes, be sure to tie them to some support so that they will not be washed overboard.

- Sitting or lying for long periods in a life raft or boat slows up circulation and results in pain and numbness of the feet, followed by swelling and later the formation of "water blisters" or ulcers called "immersion or trench foot."

- To prevent immersion foot, the following precautions are helpful: (1) Keep your craft bailed out and as dry as possible. Bail with a can or bucket or whatever you have on board. If you haven't anything else, use your hat. Next, keep the bottom dry with a sponge or piece of cloth or your undershirt; sop it up and squeeze the moisture over the side. (2) Loosen your shoe lacings, remove garters, and avoid all constrictions of clothing that in any way impair circulation of blood to the lower extremities. (3) Exercise your toes. Move as frequently as you can so that you do not become too cramped, but conserve your energy, too.

- If your feet and legs become numb and swollen, do not apply massage or heat, but keep them elevated and as dry as possible. If swelling is severe, remove your shoes.

- Take every precaution to prevent your raft from turning over. In rough weather when seas are high, keep the sea anchor out from the bow; sit low in the raft, with the passengers' weight distributed to hold the weather side down. Don't sit on the sides or stand up! Never make a sudden move without warning the other passengers. Don't tie a fishline to yourself or the raft; a large fish may capsize the raft or tow it in a different direction than you wish to go.

Fresh-Water Problem

At sea there is water everywhere, but none to drink! The fresh-water problem is as serious as it is in the desert. However, modern life rafts and boats are equipped with the latest survival kits, which even include small outfits for converting salt water into fresh water.

Lundin Lifeboat

A new and better type of lifeboat is now in use on many commercial and cruise ships. Called the Lundin decked lifeboat, this craft has a high stability rating and two may be nested within the height of one standard lifeboat when stowed on board.

Life Raft Care

Be sure that your raft is properly inflated at all times. If the main buoyancy chambers are not firm, top off with pump or mouth inflation tube. Check if air valve is open before pumping (to open, turn valve left). Cross seats should be inflated where provided, unless there are injured survivors who should lie prone.

Use caution with air valves! Don't overinflate! Air chambers should be well rounded, but not drum tight. *Be sure air valve is closed tight!* Regularly check air inflation. Remember, hot air expands, so on hot days release some of the air in the chambers. As the day or night cools off, add air.

Other Hints

Always put out a sea anchor or some kind of drag. You can improvise one from the raft case or covering, bucket, canvas or clothing or whatever is at hand. Let the anchor drag from a line from your raft. A sea anchor will help you stay more or less close to your abandoned ship or aircraft ditching site, aiding searchers. Be especially careful not to snag the raft bottom or air chambers. Keep all sharp objects such as knives, fish hooks, boathooks, ration tins and other sharp or abrasive objects off the bottom of the raft.

Water leaks are most likely to occur at valves, seams and underwater surfaces. They can be repaired with the repair plugs usually provided in life raft kits. Most life rafts have buoyancy tubes separated into two or more compartments or air chambers. If one chamber is damaged, keep the others fully inflated.

A plankton net, which should be stowed on all life-boats and rafts, can be towed behind each craft in emergency situations. In some areas several pounds of plankton can be caught in the net every few hours. Plankton is nourishing and it is full of iodine and other minerals that are beneficial to health. Most plankton caught are tiny shrimplike crustaceans or fish ova, along with fish larvae, shellfish of various species, jellyfish, miniature crabs and many varieties and colors of small sea creatures. Plankton has a noxious smell similar to strong cheese; however, its taste is not all that unpleasant. Those who have eaten it under survival conditions prefer it to roast grasshoppers, pine-bark beetles or the larvae the Indians gather at Mono Lake in California.

Navigating Your Raft

In spite of your sea anchor, your raft will drift. Do not attempt to navigate your raft unless you are within sight of land. It is too difficult to steer. The course it will head is the result of both wind and current, modified by your use of oars or paddle, tiller, sea anchor and sails.

Life rafts are not equipped with keels, so they cannot be sailed into the wind even if you are an experienced sailor. However, anyone can sail a raft downwind, and multiplace (except 20-person) rafts can be successfully sailed 10° off from the direction of the wind. Again, don't attempt to sail your craft unless you know that land is near. It will be a waste of time and energy. If the wind is blowing directly toward your plotted destination, inflate the raft fully, sit high, take in the sea anchor, rig a sail and use an oar for a rudder.

Making a Landfall

The lookout posted on watch should scan the sea in all directions for signs of land, aircraft or ships. In tropical waters a greenish tint in the sky is often caused by the reflection of sunlight from the shallow lagoons or shelves of coral reefs. In arctic regions ice fields or snow-covered land are often indicated by light-colored reflections on the clouds, quite different from the darkish gray caused by open expanses of water. Unless a tidal river is flowing into the ocean in a particular area, deep water is dark green or dark blue. Lighter color indicates shallow water, which may mean land is near.

In fog, mist, rain, snow or at night you can sometimes detect nearby land from characteristic odors and sounds, such as the musty smell of swamps and mangroves or tidal mud flats. The smell of burning wood will carry a long way off shore. The roar of surf falling on sandy beaches and rocky shores can be heard long before the surf is seen. This warning will give you time to decide whether to drift by a dangerous coastline or attempt a landing through the surf. You might judge it safer to look for a less hazardous landing farther along a coastline.

In the tropics mirages may be seen, especially during the middle of the day. Don't mistake a mirage for nearby land. A mirage characteristically will disappear or change its appearance and elevation when viewed from slightly different heights and directions.

Note the direction of birds. Usually more birds are found near land than over the open sea. The direction from which flocks fly at dawn and to which they fly at dusk may indicate the direction of nearby land. Naturally, during the day the birds are searching for food and the direction of flight has no significance.

Getting Ashore

If you are forced to swim ashore, wear your shoes and at least one thickness of clothing. In unfamiliar waters use the side or breast stroke to conserve strength.

- If the surf is moderate, ride in on the back of a small wave by swimming forward with it. Shallow dive to end your ride just before the wave breaks.

- For safety reasons, in a high surf you should swim shoreward in the trough between waves. After a "big" wave passes, work your way shoreward in the next trough.

- If you are caught in the undertow of a large wave, push up off the bottom or swim to the surface and proceed shoreward as above.

- If you are forced to land on a rocky coast, look for a place where the waves rush up into the rocks. Avoid places where the waves explode with a high white spray. Years ago, I nearly drowned in a spot like this up in Alaska when I volunteered to take a line ashore from a disabled USC&GS vessel.

- After selecting your landing point, swim slowly in making your approach—you will need your strength to hold onto the rocks. Swim behind a large wave into the breakers. Face forward and take a sitting position with your feet in front, two or three feet lower than your head, so that your feet will absorb shocks when you land or strike submerged boulders and reefs. (This is the reason you should have your shoes on when landing!)

- If you can't reach shore behind the wave you have chosen, swim with your hands only. As the next wave approaches, take a sitting position, with feet forward. Repeat procedure until you land. Try to keep from being pitched forward onto your face and stomach when assuming the face-and-feet-forward position.

- Stay off seaweed areas if possible. If this is impos-

sible, crawl over the top by grasping the vegetation with overhand swimming movements.
- Cross rocky reefs just as you would land on a rocky shore, as mentioned above.

Rafting Ashore

If you have to go through surf to reach shore, take down the raft mast, canvas, windshields or canopies. Keep your clothes and shoes on to avoid severe rock cuts and abrasions. Adjust and inflate your life jacket. Trail the sea anchor over the stern with as much line as you have to keep you headed in at right angles or directly head-on into the beach. Use the oars or paddles constantly to keep the craft under control; keep your raft pointed toward shore. Paddling prevents the sea from throwing the stern around and capsizing you. Ride in on the seaward side of a large wave.

Against a strong offshore wind, with heavy surf, the raft must have all the speed possible to pass rapidly through the oncoming crest to avoid being turned broadside, or from pitch-poling or being thrown end over end. If possible, stand off the surf a few minutes and watch the waves before attempting to pass through. Generally, every third or fifth wave will swell and crest higher than the others. If possible, avoid meeting a large wave at the moment it breaks.

In medium surf, with no on- or offshore wind, keep the raft from passing over a wave so rapidly that it drops suddenly after topping the crest. If the raft capsizes, try to grab hold of the handline that surrounds the edge or gunwale.

Ride in onto the beach as far as you can. Don't jump out of the raft until it has grounded. Then get out quickly and beach it above the highwater mark. Make the raft fast to a rock, brush or tree so that the wind will not blow it back into the water! If possible, don't land at night. If you believe that the shore is inhabited, lay away from the beach and anchor outside the surf until daylight. Signal and wait for the people on land to come out and bring you in.

14

Hot Weather and Desert Survival

With the great increase in recreational leisure time, more people are traveling the desert trails than ever before. Rock hounds, uranium hunters, prospectors, camera-bugs, campers and hunters are heading out into remote sections of primitive desert in all types of mobile equipment.

Death Valley, the Mojave and Colorado deserts in the United States and the Sonoran desert in Mexico can be just as terrifying under survival conditions as any other desert in the world. The desert in the Southwest is characterized generally by brilliant sunshine, a wide temperature range (here the temperatures during summer can soar to 136° F. in the shade with surface temperatures sometimes in excess of 156° F.), sparse vegetation, a scarcity of water, a high rate of evaporation and low annual rainfall. Some areas are flat and sandy, some mountainous and rocky, and others may be salt marshes or dunes.

The extremes in desert formation are in California. In the Mojave desert, for instance, within a 40-mile radius, elevations vary considerably. Bad Water in Death Valley National Monument at 282 feet below sea level is only 40 linear miles from the great treeless desert of granite near the top of Mount Whitney at an elevation of 14,496 feet, the highest peak in the United States outside of Alaska.

A Word of Caution

Travel in the desert can be an interesting and enjoyable experience or it can be a fatal or nearly fatal nightmare. The desert can be beautiful, but deadly. Danger is always present once you leave well-traveled roads. Not only strangers and Sunday sightseers have found this to be true, many native-born desert rats have also had tragic accidents. Don't fear this great recreational area, but respect it. Before traveling into the desert, learn the basic principles of outdoorsmanship and self reliance.

Be Prepared

The preliminary planning for desert camping is the same as for all camping. Organize and plan your desert jaunt well in advance. This gives you time to make any changes in route or personnel.

Be sure that your vehicle is in excellent mechanical condition; that all persons going on the trek are in good health, with no major problems; that you have sufficient rations and food to last throughout the trip.

You will need to know how to read a map, how to use your compass, how to find your direction by the stars, how to locate yourself if you should become lost and how to signal for help. In other words, you need to have absorbed all the information in the earlier chapters in this book on orienting yourself, map reading, compass use, star gazing and signaling.

You should also study the chapter on Woodcraft for you may need to know how to build a shelter, how to trap or snare animals, build a fire and cook.

Do not go into the desert without the know-how of survival. The desert is no easier a place for a tenderfoot to live than the Arctic. And heat can kill as fast as extreme cold.

Have some skills at your command so that if you get lost, if your vehicle breaks down, or a member of your party is injured, you will have an adventure rather than a nightmare.

Take enough water. Don't depend on water holes. They may be dry. Carry enough water to get you to your destination and back again.

To have a safe experience in the desert, everything you do, each motion you make and each step you take must be preceded by the thought: Am I safe doing this?

Checking with Officials

Be sure to leave word with your family and friends about where you are going and where you will leave the main highway. Tell local desert officials where you are going and how long you plan to be away. Be sure to check in at the sheriff's substation or ranger station on your return, otherwise a costly search and rescue action may ensue.

Don't hesitate to ask advice from desert officials. Heed their suggestions. They know and patrol the vast desert domain, but are spread very thin and do not get into all sections sometimes for months. They are there to help in time of need.

Sand dunes in the desert. The experienced or inexperienced outdoorsman must each be prepared before entering such an environment.

Stick to your route. If you don't, precious hours and even days may be wasted looking for you in the area you reported you were going to but didn't.

Obey all road and trail signs. They mean what they say!

Desert Hazards

Wind is probably the biggest threat to desert enjoyment. Camping in sites protected by mesquite trees or rocks will minimize the problem. Tents with external frames stand up better than those with poles inside. You should carry extra cord to guy the tent, and pitch it facing away from the wind to avoid a wind-scoop effect. Camp vehicles offer ideal protection (however, this is not true of pop-up tent trailers, which are highly vulnerable to strong winds).

Your Car in the Desert

Distances are great and service is scarce. While crossing the desert is not a safari into the hostile unknown unless you seek out the hinterlands, you should be sure your engine is in top condition. Watch the gas gauge and plan fill-ups accordingly. Quality tires in good condition are important during the summer, on or off the pavement, to avoid overheating and blowouts.

Vapor lock often keeps an overheated engine from restarting after a brief stop. The only solution is to wait for it to cool, although you can speed the process by wrapping a wet cloth around the fuel pump.

When the gauge shows that the car is heating, stop, preferably with the radiator facing into the wind, and keep the engine running faster than at idle. Turn off the air conditioner if you have one. Turning off the motor stops circulation in the radiator, and it may boil. Don't remove the cap. Overheated radiators erupt like geysers.

If you explore beyond the highway or established dirt roads, beware of the tracks made by jeeps and dune buggies. These tracks look like passable roads but they often lead to trouble for an ordinary car.

On an unknown poor road, avoid going downhill through sand or gravel unless you know how you can get back up or that there is an alternative route cut. The rule is: explore upgrade but not downgrade.

Give up quickly if you start to get stuck. Spinning the wheels in sand or gravel only digs the car in deeper.

If stuck, traction can be increased by letting from five to ten pounds of air pressure out of the tires. Then be sure to pump them back up (carry a tire pump and pressure gauge) or drive slowly—under 20 m.p.h. even on the highway.

Start, stop and turn gradually as sudden motions cause wheels to dig in.

If reducing the air pressure doesn't work, use an axle jack to lift each wheel six or eight inches and place stones, brush, or boards underneath the tires.

If you plan to drive in the desert, practice "difficult traction" in a dry wash with another car standing by to tow you out if you become stuck. Experiment with the various footings.

If in doubt of the terrain, get out of the car and check it out first on foot. Do not attempt to negotiate washes without first checking the footing and the clearances. High centers may rupture the oil pan of the car. Overhang may cause the driving wheels to become suspended above the ground.

Dust

If you run into a sudden cloud of dust on the road, it may be a "dust devil"—a miniature whirlwind. Slow down and turn on your headlights, even in daytime. The dust cloud may confuse drivers coming the other way, but if they can see your lights, they'll know they should keep to their lane and away from you.

Gusty Winds

The sudden impact of harsh winter winds can be deadly if you're towing a trailer or driving a camper truck. The wind will make a trailer feel light as it leans and lifts from the pavement. A camper truck will unexpectedly try to jump lanes.

To avoid disaster, slow to thirty miles an hour, or even to twenty. If your vehicle regains stability, make for the nearest telephone and phone the local sheriff's office for a wind advisory. If you're told that the roads haven't been ordered closed yet for campers or trailers, you'll know you can proceed, but at reduced speed.

Temperatures

From March through October it may be hot on the low desert (100° to 120° F.), but will usually cool at night. A man without water can die in one day under these circumstances, but there is no reason to be in such a predicament. Even if stranded, unless in the most remote sections where only the experienced and knowledgeable should venture, wait at your car until help comes. Through the winter season, occasional cold days and freezing nights are more of a hazard than heat. Temperatures usually stay balmy through fall, winter and spring, but be sure to have jackets and warm sleeping bags along for use at night.

Flash Floods

Triggered by torrential rains, floods represent another unexpected hazard, even in desert country. In this case, too, evasive action is best. In flat, open country, you should try to outrun the onrushing water. If you can't, turn directly into it, and roll the windows up tight. When your car goes straight into a flood, it offers the least resistance. But if you allow it to be hit broadside, it's almost sure to be toppled and swept away.

If caught in a canyon or hill area, try to drive quickly to higher elevation!

Equipment

If you intend to drive off the main roads, you will need: one or more shovels, a pick-mattock, a tow chain or cable, at least fifty feet of strong nylon tow rope, a tire pump, an ax, water, gas and your regular spare parts and auto tools. Choose nylon rope, rather than manila. Nylon costs more, but has twice the strength of manila, will last much longer and its elasticity is highly desirable in extracting stuck vehicles. A ¾-inch nylon rope has a working strength of about 2,000 pounds and a breaking strength of about 10,000 pounds.

Navigational Hazards

The heat and high evaporation rate of the desert cause a phenomenon known as "mirage." The varying density distribution of the layers of hot air, usually close to the earth's surface, causes light rays to reach the observer along several paths causing distorted, multiple or sometimes inverted images. These heat waves hamper your vision, making it difficult to determine distance or objects. It may cause objects or landmarks to change shape, disappear or cause them all to appear alike.

Another type of mirage is the false dawn of the desert, which seems to make the sun rise in the west.

Ground haze is a layer of warm, dusty air close to the ground which hampers vision.

Walking

There are special rules and techniques for walking in the desert. By walking slowly and resting about ten minutes per hour, a man in good physical condition can cover between twelve and eighteen miles per day— fewer, after he becomes fatigued or lacks sufficient water or food.

Consider walking at night. It is cooler, and if lack of water is a problem you will dehydrate less. You can navigate by the stars. The disadvantages are that you cannot see well and may stumble, or you might overlook water and food sources and habitation. On the hot desert it is best to travel in the early morning or late evenings, spending midday in whatever shade may be available. The position of the sun early and late in the day will give you a better sense of direction.

When walking, choose the easiest and safest way. Go around obstacles, not over them. Instead of going up or down steep slopes, zigzag to prevent overexertion. Go around gullies and canyons instead of through them.

Use a steady, easy step. When going down hill, bend the knees considerably. Climbing, place the whole foot on the ground at one time, not the heel alone. Walking in sand, lean well forward, keeping the knees bent. On long walks do not swing your arms, but grasp the shoulder straps of your pack or your shirt at the shoulder seams to prevent your hands and lower arms from swelling.

When walking with companions, adjust your rate to the slowest man. Keep together but allow about ten feet between members.

During rest stops, sit in the shade and prop your feet up high. Remove your shoes and change socks, or straighten out the ones you are wearing. If the ground is too hot to sit on so that you cannot raise your feet, do not remove your shoes as you may not be able to get them back onto swollen feet. However, unlace your boots and adjust your socks.

CLOTHING

Clothing requirements will vary considerably with the season and the environment. For the hot desert, wear lightweight and light colored clothing that covers the entire body. Long trousers and long sleeves protect you from the sun, help to prevent dehydration and protect against insects, abrasions and lacerations by rocks and brush, and tend to reduce infections caused by these injuries. Headgear should provide all around shade as well as eye shade and shoes should be lightweight but sturdy and should protect the ankles. Remember thorns and spines make walking a problem. Woolen socks are recommended; and you should always carry spare socks. Gloves are helpful to protect hands from spines and thorns when handling brush and firewood.

Winter clothing requirements for the Southwest vary with the altitudes in which you are operating. In winter, keeping dry is important. The "layer" system is best. Several light garments are easily carried and are more versatile in varying temperatures than are heavier garments, and will be as warm. Keep in mind that other clothing may be placed over or under them. A lightweight, water repellent windbreaker should be carried to wear alone or over the layers. A coat style is best as it will protect your hips. Headgear should shade the eyes, and you should try to protect your ears. Many hats have earflaps. Footgear should be sturdy, protect the ankles, and be water repellent.

Do not grease shoes—it makes them cold, tends to rot the leather, and does not waterproof them. In winter it is important to keep the feet dry to help prevent "trench foot" and frostbite. Damp socks can be carried inside the shirt front against the body to dry them out.

Equipment

Your method of travel will dictate in large part the equipment to carry. When traveling by auto you will carry "pioneer" gear such as shovels, picks, heavy rope, etc. You must also think about bedding, cooking gear, a can opener, eating utensils, a flashlight with spare batteries, lantern with fuel, first aid kit, towels, soap, toilet paper, tissues, napkins, old newspapers.

There are many small items that can be fitted in a tobacco tin, a Band-Aid box or a similar plastic box and be ready to go at any time. Check it from time to time to be sure all items are in good condition.

Other items you should carry are: a sharp belt-knife, a good map of the area, thirty or more feet of nylon parachute shroud line, a canteen, watch, snake bite kit, and a gun and ammunition. Carry your gear in a small rucksack or pack over your shoulders. Weight carried in this manner is less tiring than if carried in your pockets or hung on your belt. The pack can be used to sit on. Also, in case of a fall, you will be safer with things like the knife and hatchet on your back, rather than at your waist.

HEALTH HAZARDS

In the desert you must protect your health and well-being, and avoid fatigue and injury because medical assistance will be some time and distance away, and because conditions are usually different and distinct from your everyday living. The desert is usually a healthy environment because of its dryness, the absence of human and animal wastes, and the sterilizing effect of the hot sun.

If you are walking or active, rest ten minutes each hour. Drink plenty of water, especially early in the morning while the temperature is still low.

While on the desert, wear sunglases to protect your eyes from glare. Even though the glare does not seem to bother you, it will impair your distance vision and retard your adaptation to night conditions. If you have no glasses, make an eyeshade by slitting a piece of paper, cardboard or cloth. Apply charcoal or soot around your eyes.

Use chapstick or grease on your lips and nostrils. Do not lick your lips if they are dry as this will hasten splitting.

Change your socks regularly even though you must change to socks you have already worn. Sun and aerate socks and underclothing to freshen them.

Do not remove your clothing in an attempt to keep cool. This will only hasten dehydration. So will sitting on the hot ground.

In winter, do not sit down if your clothing is damp or if you have been perspiring unless you have additional clothing or a fire. If you have neither, walk slowly around a tree or in a circle where the ground is level and footing good until you dry out.

Do not travel in storms. Mark the direction you were traveling and find shelter. In dust storms lie down with your back to the wind. Cover your head with a cloth to keep dust out of your eyes, ears, nose and mouth. If driving, turn on the lights and stop. Get off the road if possible to avoid collision. Back into the wind to prevent sand pitting the windshield.

Dehydration

An increase in body temperature of six to eight degrees above normal (98.6° F.) for any extended period causes death. Body temperature in a healthy person can be raised to the danger point either by absorbing heat or by generating it. The body absorbs heat from the air if the air is above 92° F. Direct sunlight striking the body will increase temperature even if the air is cool. You can also absorb heat reflected from the ground or absorb it directly from the ground by contact. Any kind of work or exercise increases body heat.

The body gets rid of excess heat and attempts to keep the temperature normal by sweating, but when you sweat the body loses water and dehydration results. It has been proven that you can do twice as much work or walk twice as far with sufficient water and a normal temperature as you can after you lose 1½ quarts of water by sweating under a 100 degree temperature.

No permanent harm is done to a man who dehydrates up to ten percent of his weight, IF, later, he drinks enough water to gain it back. However, twenty-five percent dehydration at temperatures in the nineties or above will probably be fatal. You can drink cool or warm water as fast as you want, but ice cold water may cause distress and cramps.

SYMPTOMS Only by being able to recognize the initial symptoms of dehydration can one logically expect to take corrective measures to prevent further (and possibly fatal) dehydration. Learn these symptoms:

Thirst discomfort, slow motion, no appetite, and later nausea, drowsiness and high temperature.

If dehydration is from six to ten percent, symptoms will be: dizziness, headache, dry mouth, difficulty in breathing, tingling in arms and legs, bluish color, indistinct speech and finally, inability to walk.

PREVENTION OF DEHYDRATION. Thirst is not an indication of the amount of water you need. If you drink only enough to satisfy your thirst, you can still dehydrate. Drink plenty of water, especially at mealtime and during the cooler early morning hours.

A pebble or small coin carried in your mouth will alleviate the sensation of thirst, but is not a substitute for water and will not aid in keeping your body temperature normal. Do not smoke, as it encourages oral breathing exposing large areas of mucous membrane to drying influences, thereby increasing the rate of dehydration and need for water.

Salt will do you definite harm unless you drink plenty of water. Don't worry about salt but do try to keep up the water intake.

Ration Sweat, Not Water

In hot deserts you need about a gallon of water a day. If you walk at night, you may get twenty miles for that gallon, but if you walk in the daytime heat, you will get less than ten miles to the gallon.

Keep your clothing on, including your shirt and hat. Clothing helps ration your sweat by slowing down the evaporation rate and prolonging the cooling effect. It also keeps out the hot desert air and reflects the heat of the sun. Stay in the shade during the day. Sit on something twelve or more inches off the ground, if possible. Do not lie on the ground as it can be thirty degrees hotter there than a foot above the ground. If travel is necessary, travel slowly and steadily.

Rationing water at high temperatures is actually inviting disaster because small amounts will not prevent dehydration. IT IS THE WATER IN YOUR BODY THAT MAINTAINS YOUR LIFE, NOT THE WATER IN YOUR CANTEEN.

Keep your mouth shut and breathe through your nose to reduce water loss and the drying of mucous membranes. Avoid conversation for the same reason. If possible, cover your lips with grease or oil.

Alcohol in any form is to be avoided as it will accelerate dehydration. Consider alcohol as food and not as water since additional water is required to assimilate the alcohol. For the same reason, food intake should be kept to a minimum if water is scarce.

Carrying Water

When traveling give your water supply extra thought. Carry the amount of water you will need based on the charted requirements. Do not carry water in glass containers. These may break. Metal insulated containers are good, but heavy. Carry some water in gallon or half-gallon plastic containers similar to those containing bleach. They are unbreakable, lightweight and carrying several will assure a water supply if one is damaged.

Finding Water in the Desert

If you are near water remain there and prepare signals for your rescuers. If no water is at hand look for it, following these leads:

Watch for desert trails—following them may lead to water or civilization, particularly if several such trails join and "arrow" downward toward a specific location.

Flocks of birds circle over water holes. Listen for their chirping in the morning and evening, and you may be able to locate their watering spot. Quail fly toward water in the late afternoon and away in the morning. Doves flock toward watering spots morning and evening. Also look for the diggings and browsings of wild animals as they feed near water.

Water may be found at the base of rock cliffs after a rain. It collects in the waste rock at the base of cliffs or in the gravel-wash from mountain valleys which get regular seasonal rains. Limestone and lava have more and larger springs than any other rocks. Springs of cold water are safest.

Limestone caverns often have springs, but exploring caverns is dangerous as you may get lost.

Look for springs along walls of valleys that cross the lava flow. Springs may be found along valley floors or down along their sloping sides. See if there is seepage where the dry canyon cuts through a layer of porous sandstone.

Dry stream beds may have water just below the surface. Look at the lowest point on the outside of a bend in the stream channel. Dig until you hit wet sand. Water will seep out of the sand into the hole. Damp surface sand marks a place to dig a shallow well. Dig at the lowest point and go down three to six feet. If the sand stays damp, keep digging.

Look at hillsides to see where the grass is lush and green. Dig at the base of the green zone and wait for water to seep into the hole.

Water is more abundant and easier to find in loose sediment than in rocks. Look for a wet spot on the surface of a clay bluff or at the foot of the bluff and try digging it out.

Look for the "indicator" plants which grow only where there is water: cottonwoods, sycamores, willows, hackberry, saltcedar (tamarisk), cattails and arrow weed. You may have to dig to find this water.

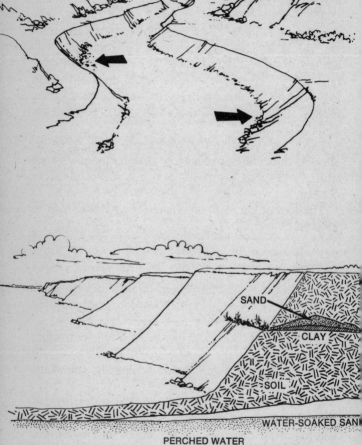

SAND

CLAY

SOIL

WATER-SOAKED SAND

PERCHED WATER

Where to look for water in the desert. Above, in a dry river or stream bed. Below, on a hillside at the base of a green zone.

Also keep on the lookout for windmills and water tanks built by ranchers.

If cactus fruits are ripe, eat a lot of them (see the chapter on plant foods), to help prevent dehydration.

The immature flower stalks of agave, yucca, and sotol contain moisture, or, if no flower stalks are present, the main stalks may be split open and the pith chewed to prevent dehydration. The barrel cactus contains a high degree of moisture, but to press out water is pure myth, as the mucilaginous, acrid juice thickens rapidly. To remove moisture chew on the pith but do not swallow it.

Carry chunks of the pith with you to suck on to alleviate thirst. Young plants six to eighteen inches high with a soft green color will have the higher moisture content.

The root of the night blooming cereus is also high in moisture.

Methods of Purifying Water

Dirty water should be filtered through several layers of cloth and allowed to settle. This does not purify the water even though it may look clean. Incidentally, radioactive fallout is dirt and can be removed from water as above.

Purification to kill germs must be done by one of the following methods:

1. Water purification tablets are the easiest to use. Get them from the drugstore before you go to desert and follow the directions on the label. Not only do you need them in your survival kit and in your car or plane, but you should keep an emergency supply at home. Generally, one tablet is sufficient for one quart of clear

water or two tablets for cloudy water. Let the water stand for thirty minutes before using.

2. Tincture of iodine. Add three drops per quart of clear water, double for cloudy water. Let stand for thirty minutes.

3. Household bleach (5.25 percent sodium hypochlorite): two drops per quart of clear water, four drops per quart of cloudy water. Stir, let stand thirty minutes. The water will have a slight chlorine taste.

4. Boiling for three to five minutes will purify most water. Add charcoal while boiling to remove disagreeable colors from water. Agitate to aerate and restore taste or add a small pinch of salt.

Desert Still

An interesting method of acquiring water is through the use of a solar still constructed as shown. The sun's rays heat the ground inside the hole, causing evaporation of the soil's moisture, which saturates the air space and condenses on the cooler plastic surface. This method will produce some water in even the driest areas, but by selecting a site where there are indications of moisture—greener plant life, loam soil, damp sand, etc.—about two to three pints per day may be obtained. Several such stills would have to be constructed to provide the amount necessary for continued survival. Cacti and other plants which contain moisture may be broken up and placed in the hole to provide a higher

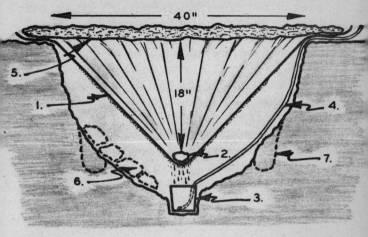

Desert Solar Still. To collect water in the desert, use a solar still. Heat from the sun vaporizes the ground moisture, which condenses under the plastic cover and trickles down into the container.

1. *Sheet of wettable plastic, 6-foot diameter.*
2. *Smooth, fist-sized rock for forming cone of plastic.*
3. *Pail, jar or cone of foil, plastic or canvas to catch water.*
4. *Drinking tube, ¼-inch plastic, about 5 feet long. (This is not absolutely necessary.)*
5. *Soil to weight plastic sheet and seal in place. A good closure is important.*
6. *Line hole with broken cacti or other succulents.*
7. *If non-potable water is available, dig a soaking trough around inside of hole. Carefully fill the trough to prevent impure water from running down and contaminating the water-catching container.*

water recovery rate. Saguaro, barrel and prickly pear cacti are best for this purpose. Nonpotable water may be poured into a trench around the inside of the hole and be distilled, and made safe for drinking by this process. If nonpotable water or plant materials are placed in the hole, be sure that they do not come in direct contact with the plastic, as the water forming on it then would be contaminated.

The basic requirement for constructing the still is a six-foot square or circular sheet or "wettable" plastic. The plastic material should be a thin tough, rough-surfaced type, of which duPont's "Tedlar" is an example. Smooth plastics are less "wettable" and the droplets forming will not adhere and run down to the point of the cone before dropping off. If a smooth type must be used, slight abrasing with scouring powder, fine sand or sandpaper will improve its wettability. Be sure the roughened side is placed down. A wide-mouth container of some kind should be used to collect the distilled water.

The site must be in full sunshine, although an established still will produce some water during the night. The hole may be dug with a sharp rock or stick, and soil removed by hand if a shovel is not available. If the container catching the water is not rigid, the bottom of the hole must be shaped to support the container as it becomes filled.

The still may become a source of food, as lizards, snakes and small animals will fall into the cone and become trapped.

FOOD

You must have water to survive, but you can go without food for some days without harmful effects.

In fact, if water is not available, do not eat, as food will only increase your need for water.

The important thing about locating food in a survival situation is to know what foods are available in your particular environment and how to obtain them.

Hawks soaring overhead may mean rabbits or other rodents below; birds flocking may mean not only edible berries but probably will mean water nearby. Game will be found around water holes and in areas with heavier bush growth.

Edible Wildlife

Almost every animal and reptile, and many insects are edible, and many are sources of highly esteemed foods. Learn how to prepare the various things that would be available to you in a survival situation. Avoid any small mammal which appears to be sick as it may have tularemia, a disease transmittable to humans. A spotted liver in the animal is also an indication of this disease. Some animals have scent glands which must be removed before cooking. Do not allow the hair of these animals to come in contact with the flesh as it will give the meat a disagreeable taste.

Preserving Surplus Meat

It is surprisingly easy to preserve surplus meats in the southwest desert because of the bright sun and dry heat. You can make *charqui* (jerky) from fat free meat of large animals, by slicing it into strips about one inch thick by several inches wide, and hanging it in the sun for two or three days until it is completely dry. It may be eaten dry or soaked and cooked. It will keep indefinitely.

Sand dried meat is similarly stripped, then wiped

dry and buried, unsalted, in dry sand about six inches deep. If kept dry it will keep for several years. Eat it dry or soak it and cook.

Smoke drying is also simple. Build a lattice about three feet above a slow burning fire, lay ¼-inch thick strips of meat on the lattice. Smoke until the meat becomes brittle. Do not let the fire become so hot that the meat cooks or draws juices—the smoke does the trick. Do not use pitchy or oily woods as they will flavor the meat.

Snares, Traps, Deadfalls

Learn to design and use these from the chapter on meat. Most are simple devices which require only ingenuity, a pocket knife, a bent nail and a piece of string. You will have these things in your survival kit— or you may have to improvise. Snares should be placed after camp is set up, but before dark. A twitch-up snare jerks the animal into the air, kills promptly and protects it against other animals. A noose of string laid around a hole or burrow can be jerked by hand as the animal puts its head out of the hole. Conceal yourself some distance away so that the animal in the hole cannot see you. Deadfalls are traps which allow a heavy object, log or rock to drop on the animal when a trigger is released. Any size animal may be killed by this method if the trap is large enough. Slings or slingshots may be used to kill birds or small animals. A handful of pea-sized rocks flung by hand may stun a bird.

Set snares in game trails or frequently used runways which you can recognize by fresh tracks and droppings. The spot used for butchering will attract other animals and will be a good place to watch for a day or so. Use entrails for bait. Place the snare in the narrowest part of the trail, or arrange obstacles to force the animal to pass through the snare. Disturb the natural surroundings as little as possible. Be sure the noose is large enough so that the head but not the body of the animal will pass through.

Plants

The main desert edibles are the fruits of cacti and legumes. All cactus fruits are safe to eat. In the summer the fleshy and thin-walled ripe fruits can be singed over fire to remove spines. Then they can be peeled and eaten.

Old cactus fruits contain seeds which can be pounded between two stones into a powder and eaten, or mixed with water into a gruel called pinole. New, young pads of the prickly pear can be singed, peeled and boiled.

The legumes are the bean bearing plants. The main ones are the honey and screwbean mesquites, the palo verde, the tesota (ironwood) and the catclaw acacia. All are small trees with fern-like leaves.

The palo verde is recognized by its open growth, greenish bark and feathery leaves. Ironwood has rough, dense growth, and will grow into a large tree under favorable conditions. Catclaw is a small, grayish tree with numerous short curved thorns. All have bean pods, which, when green and tender, can be boiled and eaten. Dry, mature beans, like cactus seeds, are too hard to chew and must be cracked to be digested.

The night blooming cereus looks like a cluster of weather-beaten sticks and is found close to trees and bushes. It has a large, edible, beetlike root. Slice the root and fry. This root has a very high moisture content, and may be used as a water source, as noted before.

Other edibles are the fruits of: the tomatillo or squawberry, a stiff thorny bush with small berries which are rather citric-tasting and much liked by birds; the hackberry, a small tree with tiny thick-growing round-ish leaves and small red berries; jojoba (the goatnut or wild hazel), a smallish shrub, with thick-growing acornlike nuts, were once a staple food of the Indians. In less arid areas, burdock, cattails, dandelions, dock, lambs-quarters, miner's lettuce, nettles (young) and water cress are a few of the more desirable edible plants. Acorns may be dangerous if eaten in large quantities. Pinion nuts, pine kernels, red berries and the young bark of aspen, cottonwood, pine and spruce are all edible.

Poisonous Plants

The identification of all poisonous plants in the Southwest is beyond the scope of this handbook. There are more than 700 in the United States and Canada. The reader is encouraged to study the matter further based on his degree of interest. There is no pattern of geography, habitat, relationship, seasonal appearance or plant part that can be used successfully to separate poisonous plants from the harmless ones.

In a survival situation where strange plants must be gathered for food, follow these rules:

Avoid plants with milky sap.

Avoid all red beans.

If possible, boil plants that are questionable.

Test a cooked plant by holding a small quantity in the mouth for a few moments. If the taste is disagree-able (very bitter, nauseating, burning), do not eat it.

Cactus Spines

Don't touch them. If you need to eat prickly pears,

use a stick to spear them or knock them off. Burn the spikes from all spiny plants and fruit and scrape off with a knife or a thin piece of stone. Then peel and eat.

Fires and Cooking

Clear an area about fifteen feet across, dig a pit or arrange rocks to contain the fire. Make a starting fire of dry grass, small twigs, shavings, under bark or cottonwoods, etc. Place larger twigs—about pencil size —on top. Have heavier material ready to add, using the smaller pieces first. Place them on the fire in a "tepee" fashion to prevent smothering your fire, and to aid in the formation of an up-draft. (See the chapter on fires.) After the fire is burning well, continue to use the tepee method for boiling, but criss-cross fuel for forming coals for frying or broiling.

Start your fire with a lighter, matches or a hand lens. Remember, do not use up your waterproofed matches unless your rescue from the desert is a guaranteed fact.

If you have aluminum foil with you, wrap your food in it, double fold the edges, leaving some air space and place it on the coals.

You can boil water or make soup in a cardboard, bark or other container of flammable material, provided you use a low fire, and keep liquid inside of the container. The part of the container above the water line may burn if not kept moist.

Poisonous Creatures

There is probably more false information about poisonous creatures than any other subject. These animals and insects are for the most part shy, or due to their nature, not often seen. Therefore, any person who has the fortune or misfortune to become acquainted with them becomes an expert, and in due course, the stories become distorted. Like gossip, the final tale seldom resembles the original fact. Learn the facts about these creatures and you will see that they are not to be feared, but only respected. Visit the museums which have displays, dead or alive, of the creatures—avoid the roadside zoos with their sensational imports if you are looking for facts.

Snakes

There are many types of snakes in the Southwest but only rattlesnakes and coral snakes are poisonous. (Sidewinders are small rattlesnakes which get their name from the peculiar side-looping method used in moving over sandy areas.) Snakes hibernate during the colder months, but will start appearing with the warming trend, sometimes in early February. During the spring and fall months they may be found in the daytime, but during the summer months they will generally be out at night, because they cannot stand excessive heat.

Rattlesnakes

Rattlesnakes are easily identified by the sandy color, the broad arrowshaped head, blunt tipped-up nose and rattles on the tail. Look for them where food, water and protection are available—around abandoned structures, irrigation ditches, water holes, brush and rock piles. They do not always give warning by rattling, nor do they always strike if one is close. Usually they are not aggressive and will not chase people. They may attempt to escape from noise and commotion, or they may remain quiet and hidden.

Rattlesnakes strike by rapidly extending the neck and upper body loops for a distance one-third to one-half their total length. The poison is injected through two curved hollow fangs which are hinged forward by the wide opening of the mouth. The strike results in immediate pain accompanied by swelling. The venom primarily causes local and internal destruction and nerve damage. Severe infection is a possibility. About ninety-nine percent of snake bites are in lower parts of the limbs.

If traveling in areas where rattlers are, wear boots and watch where you put your hands and feet. Improvised puttees of corrugated cardboard or thick newspapers underneath trousers provide effective leg protection.

If bitten, try to capture the snake as its identification will aid in specific medical treatment.

Coral Snake

A small snake, rarely over twenty inches long with a small, blunt, black head and tapering tail. Wide red and black bands are separated by narrower yellow bands completely encircling the body. They are nocturnal and live under objects, in burrows, and are shy and timid.

Corals bite and chew rather than strike, but due to their very small mouth and short fixed fangs, they are unable to bite any but the smallest extremities. Coral snakes will bite under severe provocation. The venom affects the nervous system causing failure of the heart and respiratory muscles. Wyeth Corporation, manufacturer of rattlesnake antivenin, also produces a coral snake antivenin.

Treatment of Poisonous Snakebite

If ice is available, use the Stahnke Ligature-Cryo-therapy method as follows:

1. Keep the victim quiet. Immediately apply a liga-ture (constricting band) of strong string or shoe lace between the bite and the body, just above the punctures. Tighten only until first pain is felt. If possible, place a piece of ice on the bite. Instead of ice, Frigiderm or other spray refrigerant may be used. Do not spray di-rectly on the skin. Cover the site with a thin wet cloth pad and spray with refrigerant to form ice. Respray as required to maintain an effective ice-pack.

2. Prepare a suitable vessel of crushed ice and water, and submerge the entire limb to well above the site.

3. After about ten minutes remove the ligature. Keep the limb in ice water for at least two hours.

4. Transfer the limb to a vessel of crushed ice (use no salt) for a minimum of twenty-four hours. Several days of treatment may be required for the bites of larger snakes. Ice must not be permitted to melt away from the body surfaces. If the bite is on the torso or at a point of attachment of limb to body, the entire limb and body area well above the point of attachment must be packed in ice.

5. Keep the patient comfortably warm during the first twenty-four hours. Then, until treatment is dis-continued, keep the patient warm to the point of mild perspiration. This is important to prevent tissue de-terioration. It is also very important that the patient's fluid intake be increased during treatment.

6. Hypothermia, as this ice treatment is called, must

be discontinued gradually. This is best done by again placing the member in ice water from which the ice has been removed, and permitting both to return gradually to room temperature.

Cut and Suck Method

Recent studies of the cut and suck method are showing that the technique is of doubtful value. Of about 6,000 persons bitten by poisonous snakes in the U. S. each year only about twelve die and many of the survivors had no first aid treatment whatsoever. So, if ice is not available, follow these simple instructions: Keep the victim quiet. Immediately apply a ligature as in Step 1 above. Bring a doctor to the patient.

If the cut and suck method is deemed necessary, follow the instructions with the snake bite kit or in the First Aid Chapter.

In any event, Step 1 above is very important.

To prevent excessive damage to tissues, nerves, and blood vessels, make the longer, deeper incision at right angles. The depth of cut will depend on the size of the snake and the area bitten.

Do not hesitate to suck by mouth. Venom is not a stomach poison, and the amount one would absorb through sores in the mouth would not harm you.

To be effective, the incisions must be made *immediately* after the bite, and suction applied for an hour or more. This treatment used one hour after the bite has little if any value.

Gila Monster

This is our only poisonous lizard. Due to its small numbers, it is protected by law. It is seldom over twenty inches long, with a beaded black and coral colored skin. It moves sluggishly but can swap ends and snap rapidly. The bite is poisonous (but the breath is not). The neurotoxic venom is carried from glands in the lower jaw by grooved teeth. The poison seems to be an anti-coagulant and the wounds bleed freely accompanied by swelling. Death results from heart and respiratory failure. If bitten, grab the gila behind the head and yank it off. The teeth are not set in sockets and come out readily. Use ice treatment, and get to a doctor, as fast as possible.

Poisonous Insects and Spiders

The potentially lethal species in this area are the small rock or bark scorpion, the black widow spider and the wasp. The recluse spider bite results in serious ulceration. Bites or stings of other species may be painful, but generally are not dangerous except that great hazard of infection exists in all cases.

The rock or bark scorpion is a small, very slim, light straw colored insect. The stinger in the tip of the tail injects a minute amount of powerful venom. It is dangerous to small children, the elderly and those with high blood pressure, heart or respiratory ailments. There will be pain from sting, numbness, restlessness, fever, fast pulse and breathing difficulty. Healthy adults usually have little serious reaction.

The black widow spider is a shiny black insect with red hour glass markings on the abdomen. It is found in the dark corners of sheds and outbuildings, under logs and in rock piles. It will bite if provoked. The bite can be dangerous to all ages, but is seldom fatal. Pain spreads throughout the body, accompanied by headache, dizziness and nausea. Extremities become cramped, the abdomen becomes rigid, pupils dilate and spasms may occur after several hours.

The recluse or brown spider is a light brown colored insect, about one-half inch in length, active at night. It is easily identified by the violin-shaped marking on the head and back. It is rarely found in the desert. The bite causes local reddening and swelling, and results in an ulcerous wound extremely difficult to heal.

The tarantula, giant hairy scorpion and desert centipede are not dangerous, but may inflict a painful bite or sting. A tarantula bite may produce anaphylaxis.

Ants, velvet ants, wasps and hornets may cause a painful sting, usually not serious. Application of strong household ammonia, Mrs. Stewart's liquid household bluing or ice is helpful in reducing pain and in most cases just about completely neutralizes the effects of the sting.

Conenose bugs are bloodsuckers which may inject disease-producing organisms.

The vinegaroon, solpugid and Jerusalem cricket are not only harmless, but are beneficial to man.

Prevention and Treatment

In places where various species are expected, carefully inspect all clothing and bedding before use, especially items that have been on or near the ground during the night. Dampness seems to attract these creatures. During summer evenings scorpions travel over the desert floor and up the branches of trees and bushes looking for food. Bedding on the ground will provide them with a hiding place toward morning. If bitten (stung) apply a ligature and ice. Do not cut and suck. Remove ligature after five minutes. Get to a doctor, especially if the victim is a child, is elderly, has a bad heart or has been bitten several times or on the main part of the body.

Poisonous Spines

Never try to brush away cactus spines that get into your skin, as they are likely to break off, making it difficult to pull them out. If they do break off, it means a dig and probe job with a knife or tweezers. Or, they may become infected and can be squeezed out.

If you have a first aid kit, be sure to apply an antiseptic. If infected, and you can heat water and have a bar of soap, soften the soap to a jelly consistency and soak your finger or hand in the hot soapy water every hour until the infection abates.

Rabies (Hydrophobia)

Rabies is a disease of warm-blooded animals. Domestic dogs and cats and many desert animals (coyotes, foxes, skunks, gophers, rats, bats) can transmit the disease to man by biting him. If a person is bitten by a strange animal it is important to capture and isolate it, if possible. The suspected animal must be kept in isolation for fourteen days unless its death intervenes, in which case the undamaged head should be sent to the state laboratory for examination. The victim should get to a doctor as soon as possible although the start of the treatment may be delayed for several days without danger. Untreated rabies infection is always fatal.

A special warning in regard to bats: Do not pick up or handle bats as they are believed to be the most common carriers and transmitters of the disease.

15

Shipwrecks, Crash Landings, and Other Disasters

If you happen to be a pilot forced down on a beach, a survivor from a shipwreck that has landed along a coastal area or just a lost hiker or fisherman, you will find a greater variety of edible animal and plant food along a seacoast than in any other terrain. However, survival conditions can be radically different depending upon whether you are on a subtropical shore in Florida, Puerto Rico or Mexico, or in the tropics of Central or South America. Life can be less harassing in a temperate zone along the United States and Canada, and more rugged in the subarctic and arctic seacoasts of these countries. In arctic coastal areas you will need shelter and warmth before looking for water and food. In a jungle or tropical coastal area water would be the first need, then shelter and food. In desert coastal regions, such as along Baja California, water of course would be most important, and shelter from sun and wind next.

A rule to remember: If you land on a seashore, stay close to the beach. Do not attempt to work your way inland, through forest or swamp. If you decide to travel, move along the shore rather than go inland, unless you cross a path that looks as if it leads to a village.

Driftwood Fires

Driftwood is usually plentiful along seashores, so cooking, keeping warm and lighting signal fires are not the severe problems they would be in some of the other regions, unless it is winter and the snow is heavy. Always make your camp and cooking fire in a safe place, never in a pile of driftwood where an inshore wind could cause the fire to spread for many miles inland and not only destroy valuable timber, but burn out ranches and possibly a town or two further inland.

Where to Look for Food

You should find something to eat wherever you are. Walk the beach when the tide is out to find oysters and clams living under a thin layer of sand, and dig them up.

Lobsters and crabs should be hunted by night when they move around and are easier to catch. If you bait a line with a dead fish tied just below a sinker, drag the line through the water slowly and examine it frequently to see if you have caught anything. Be prepared to stun the lobster or crab or crayfish so that it doesn't scurry back into the water away from you. Take care not to get caught in the lobster's sharp claws.

Most shellfish can be eaten raw, but are better cooked. Lobster and crabs can be cooked by boiling them alive in hot water for fifteen minutes.

Turtles and their eggs are also good food. The eggs can usually be found in the sand, at the end of small parallel tracks. To catch a turtle, rush it and turn it over on its back. All parts of a turtle are edible except the shell, the kidneys and the stomach. The meat can be boiled or baked, but it tastes better baked.

The sea cucumber, which looks like its name and is found on rocks or tropical reefs, has five long white muscles on the inside of the body that can be stripped off and boiled.

Although some sea urchins are edible, others are not, and I would not recommend eating them, for on a seashore there is enough food available so one does not have to take chances.

Fish are, of course, available if you can catch them. You might be able to cast for them using a line and bent safety pin for a hook, and pieces of fish for bait. Sometimes they can be caught by hand in small pools of water. You will probably have better luck trapping fish in shallow water using some of the improvised traps as illustrated than with any other method.

Searching for Plants

Wild foods are good foods, with high vitamin and mineral content. Fleshy-leafed plants make good salad greens; and fresh wild fruits and berries provide fluid when water supplies are low and will help to keep the intestinal tract functioning properly.

Don't worry if your bowels do not eliminate properly or if gas forms. You may even suffer for a few days with dysentery until your system becomes accustomed to the change of diet from home-cooked foods to raw or too much wild roughage.

How to Obtain Drinkable Water

Fresh-water streams emptying into the ocean may be brackish near the outlet due to salt-water tides moving up the tidal stream.

Palatable water may be obtained by digging several beach "wells." The holes should be dug a safe distance above the high tide mark and deep enough to permit water to collect in the bottom. Skim off and use only the top layer of the water after it has been allowed to settle for a few minutes. The water may still be a little brackish, but will probably not be too salty to be used. It will be safer to boil the water since the stream may be polluted from distant villages far inland or from dead animals.

You can also obtain water by the solar condensation method as outlined in the chapter on Desert Survival.

If you happen to be in a tropical zone, drinkable water or juices may be obtained from fruits such as the coconut and guava. Coconuts are the most reliable tropical source of pure water. Green nuts are better than the ripe ones for both water content and food value.

Bamboo stems sometimes have water in the hollow joints. Shake the stems of old, yellowish bamboo. If you hear a gurgling sound, cut a notch at the base of each joint and catch the water in a container or drink directly from the notch.

Many beach shrubs have long water storage roots just under the surface of the soil. When cut in long sections and held vertically, some of these roots furnish an appreciable amount of clear, palatable water. Vines are often good sources of water. Choose a good-sized vine and cut off a three- to six-foot length. Make the first cut at the top. Sharpen one end and hold a container or your mouth to the sharpened end. The water will be clear, fresh and pure.

Caution: Never drink from a vine that has milky sap!

In the American tropics in the Everglades of Florida, parts of Mexico, the East Indies and other similar regions, the large branches of trees often support air plants whose overlapping leaves may hold a considerable amount of rain water. The water should be strained through a cloth, however, to eliminate dirt, insects and other debris trapped in the leaves.

Be careful when climbing these trees, for you may find a venomous spider or snake. Frequently, you will encounter one or more edible tree frogs in the foliage.

JUNGLE SURVIVAL

Everyday commercial and private aircraft on pleasure and business trips fly over the dry and wet jungles of Florida, Mexico, Central and South America and the Far East.

Although the personnel aboard a plane are taught survival and ditching techniques, it is possible that they may all be injured or killed in a crash landing. In this situation it might just be possible that you could not only save your own life, but the lives of other survivors as well if you remember the proper jungle techniques.

To crash-land or become lost in the jungles on the North American continent can be just as terrifying as it would be in the Amazon of South America or in the tropical islands of the Far East. To survive for any length of time in a jungle there is no doubt that you will need physical stamina, high morale, survival know-how and at least the minimum of equipment.

As in other situations, a jungle survival victim must be able to secure safe drinking water, food and shelter and to make fires to cook whatever food he is able to obtain. He must be able to overcome the biological and mental hazards he will encounter before the ordeal is over.

Water-Borne Diseases

In some regions, mainly in Mexico, South America and Asia, water-borne diseases are a major hazard. Deadly amoebic dysentery and the bacillary dysentery can wear a person down so that he soon becomes too weak to travel. Typhoid, blood flukes, liver flukes and cholera are a few of the water-borne diseases found in this type of terrain. Worms and leeches can also be swallowed when drinking impure water. Beware of unboiled water obtained near or below an Indian or native village. Water-borne diseases can be carried hundreds of miles downstream. Peoples of many countries have a habit of throwing dead carcasses and just about everything else into rivers and streams to dispose of them.

If You Must Travel

In attempting to reach civilization while traveling through heavy rank vegetation or crossing vast swamps near rivers, oppressive heat and humidity can be very cruel and exhausting.

In this type of terrain laying out a compass course is impossible due to the necessity of making too many "off-sets." (See Chapter Two.) One is literally forced to chop his way through with a machete. The work is so exhausting that it is easier to follow game trails that meander along streams and rivers. This, of course,

Two fish traps that can provide varied nourishment over a long period of time. Top, *a tidal flat trap.* Bottom, *two maze-type traps that can work on tidal flats or on rivers.*

will add to your mileage. However, cutting across country can be just as trying. It is better to travel along ridges and divides wherever possible.

Dry and Wet Jungles

Water can be a problem even in a rainforest. Some jungles are very arid, others have a dry and wet season. Securing water in a jungle can be a serious problem during a dry season. Therefore, you may have to depend on some type of water-yielding plants, such as vines.

Tap a vine by cutting it off as high as you can reach. Next, cut it off at the ground level. This will give you a water tube six to eight feet long. Water will start flowing almost immediately. Some sections will produce almost a quart of pure liquid. The large jungle lianas or vines offer the best drinking water and contain the most moisture of all the plants except the coconut palm nuts.

Of course, you can solve your water problems in advance by carrying a SRL Sun Still also. (See the chapter on Desert Survival.)

Jungle Food

In general, most jungles look similar. In heavier jungles birds and animals may be scarce, so you may have to subsist mostly on plant food. Animals tend to inhabit the edges of rivers or streams where travel is easier for them. These are the areas where one can catch fish and snare small animals to better advantage.

Here are a few of the plants that are edible:

COCONUTS. Of the many varieties of plant food, the best known, perhaps, is the coconut palm tree.

Coconut palms provide both food and drink, if one is able to open them. To take the husk off the coconut, hit it against a sharpened stake set upright in the ground. Then, twist the coconut to pry off a small portion of the husk. Repeatedly hitting the husk and prying it off will eventually remove the entire husk. Underneath the husk is the nut, which can be opened just below the two eyes at the stem end by striking it with a stone.

Coconut oil is good for sunburns and as insect repellent, and it prevents salt-water sores and bloating. To obtain the oil, boil the meat in a container of fresh water. When the mixture cools, the oil will rise to the top and can be skimmed off.

Not all palm trees are coconut palms, but almost all palms provide good eating. Most of them have juicy fruits or nuts and a sweet sap. The flower stalks and flowers are edible, and the cabbage, the tender point growing at the tip of the trunk beneath the base of the leaves, can be eaten raw or cooked.

BAMBOO grows very rapidly, sometimes as much as twelve inches a day, during and after the rainy season. The young shoots, about twelve inches high, are good food and should be cooked like asparagus, that is, boiled in water until tender.

Mature bamboo stems are woody and can be used as utensils, fishing poles, knives and blowguns. Darts can be made from reeds. A wad of cotton should be tied to the base of the dart to set up compression so that when the gun is blown, the dart will be propelled from the tube.

ARROWROOT is a rainforest plant with leaves that are three feet in diameter and flowers that are purple and green. The roots of the arrowroot, often twelve inches long, are highly edible, better cooked than raw.

PAPAYA is a melonlike fruit that grows on the stem of a twenty-foot plant. The fruit is green when unripened and yellow when ripe. If milky juice comes from the rind when the papaya is cut, it is not ripe enough to be eaten and must be set in the sun for a couple of days. This same milky juice is irritating to the skin and can cause blindness.

BREADFRUIT grows on a tree about thirty feet high with large leathery ornamental leaves. The fruit hangs at the end of the branches and is about six inches thick, yellowish green and rough in texture. The skin should be scraped, and the fruit can be baked, grilled or boiled like potatoes, although the scraped fruit can be eaten raw.

SUGAR CANE can be found in uninhabited jungle and looks like a cornstalk about ten feet high, though it can grow taller. Ripe cane contains a sweet juice that can be sucked out once the outer layer of the stem is peeled away.

Terrors of the Jungle

Most of it is pure bunk! Most stories about jungle animals, snakes and spiders are just not true!

Poisonous snakes are scarcer than most people think. I have traveled considerably in the jungles of the Everglades, Mexico and parts of South America, and venomous snakes are no more prevalent there than the rattlesnake and vipers of the North American continent.

There is little danger of a bite if you wear shoes, sleep off the ground and watch where you sit or place your hands. You probably will never see a poisonous snake or a large animal. What may frighten you most are the horrible howls, screams and crashing sounds made by noisy monkeys, birds, night insects and falling trees.

Dangerous Insects

The real dangers of the jungles are the insects, many of which pass on diseases and parasites. Mosquitoes transmit malaria, an illness that will probably be your worst enemy. Mosquitoes are generally encountered from late afternoon until early morning.

To guard against bites, camp away from swamps, on high land or where a breeze will blow the insects away. If you do not have insect repellent or mosquito netting, cover your bare skin with mud, especially when you sleep at night. Tuck your pants legs into your socks or boots. If you have anti-malaria tablets, take them according to directions as long as they last. Even though you are bitten by infected mosquitoes, you won't become ill for a week or so. By that time you probably will have been rescued.

Ticks are numerous in some areas, especially in grassy places. You may get many of them on your body. Strip to the skin once or twice a day and inspect your body for ticks, leeches and other pests. If a tick attaches itself to your body, cover it with a drop of iodine or other strong disinfectant. Sometimes touching it with a lighted cigarette will make it let go if it is not too deeply imbedded. Be careful when removing a tick— the head may stay in and will start infection.

Scorpions are hazardous, for they like to hide in clothing, bedding or shoes. They will attack and strike without being touched. Spiders, scorpions and centipedes are abundant in the jungle, and some are very large and dangerous. Their sting will make you sick for a few hours.

Chiggers, wasps and wild bees are pests whose stings can be fatal in some cases. Chiggers, mites and fleas bore under the skin and cause painful sores. Usually a drop of oil or pitch will kill them. Treat ant, wasp and bee stings with cold compresses. (See First Aid chapter.)

HOW TO SURVIVE CRASH LANDINGS

Recently, the Government's safety board blamed pilot error for two-thirds of the over 5,000 private and commercial aircraft accidents. Far too many of the 120,000 family flying enthusiasts, businessmen and others have perished in forced landings while crossing over rugged terrain—not so much from the crash landing, but from exposure. The sportsman flying into remote country is prepared, for he will be dressed for the woods and will have food, hunting or fishing and camping gear in the aircraft to see him through his ordeal if he hasn't been fatally injured during the landing.

It Can Happen to You

Your engine may stop while you are crossing a rough and rugged mountain range, with no emergency landing strip or alpine meadow that you can glide down into. However, you make a successful crash landing in a wooded area and are able to crawl out unharmed. You find that you are in remote back country miles from help. The weather turns from cold rain to snow. You huddle as best you can in the shelter provided by the downed aircraft. It's not enough. Your body is found a week later by a search and rescue team. All signs indicate that you were not badly injured, but died from exposure several days after the accident. I have found several fliers' bodies with no more than a few minor scratches on them. They had frozen to death. They wore only a business suit or summer flying coveralls. These victims were not dressed or prepared for a forced landing in mountain country.

Today's pleasure aircraft are excellent and dependable and have very few mechanical difficulties. Probably because of this too many pilots become overconfident and complacent, or just plain careless. Many believe the chances are slight that they will ever be forced down beyond gliding range of some sort of emergency landing field. This is where they make their first bad mistake.

The crash landing where the flier has been able to walk away unharmed, only to perish a few days later from exposure is unnecessary. Why do people perish? Because they do not know survival technique.

How to Survive

File a flight plan and stick to it. If it becomes necessary to make a change of plan while enroute to a destination, notify FAA of this change.

If you are in range or flying over FAA facilities, call in occasionally and let them know that you are near, and give them other pertinent information you may have. In case of an emergency, it will save searchers many hours in locating you if they have a general idea of your location. If they can reach you quickly, it may save your life.

All communication stations are ready to provide pilots with enroute flight information at any time. You may call any FAA radio for latest weather reports, upper wind velocities, airport conditions and other flight information. If you become lost or uncertain of your position, call any FAA radio. Personnel at these stations are trained to assist pilots in establishing position by any of the following methods: (1) visual reference to terrain features; (2) low-frequency radio range orientation; (3) VHF OMNI-RANGE indications (triangulations).

Search and rescue is a life-saving service provided through combined efforts of the FAA, Air Force, Coast Guard and Civil Air Patrol in cooperation with other organizations such as state aeronautics authorities, sheriff's air patrol, state police, ranger service and local search and rescue units (mountain rescue teams, etc.). It provides search, survival aid and rescue of missing personnel or crashed aircraft.

All you need to remember to obtain this valuable protection is:

1. File a flight plan with FAA Airway Communications stations in person or by telephone or radio.
2. File an arrival report.
3. If you land at a location other than your intended destination, report the landing to the nearest communications station.
4. If you land enroute and are delayed more than an hour, report this information to the nearest communications center.
5. Remember that if you fail to report within an hour after your ETA, a search will be started to locate you. If you fail to report within three hours after your ETA, the full facilities of the Search and Rescue Service will be activated.

Survival Kit

Carry a good well-fitted survival kit packed into a frame knapsack. If you are forced down and have to travel afoot later, you can carry your outfit comfortably and all articles will be contained, not scattered through the aircraft. Should a crash occur, the survival kit must be tossed out of the craft quickly in case the plane catches on fire. (See pages 305–306.)

Flying over Large Bodies of Water

If you fly over large bays or vast stretches of water, include a well-equipped small rubber life raft in your

This USAF HH-3E helicopter has a 217-foot hoist cable to penetrate the jungle and hoist men through dense growth. Called the Jolly Green Giant helicopter, it has been used to rescue men in Vietnam.

equipment. It should contain a Very pistol, signal cartridges or flares, oars, sail and a sea anchor to hold the raft into the wind. A bailing bucket strung out astern will also come in handy for bailing or use as a sea anchor. In an emergency a seat cushion will serve the purpose.

Other useful items are: canned water, emergency rations, a steel signal mirror, fishhooks and line, several fish lures or nonperishable bait. Some kind of tarpaulin will be handy to shield you from the hot sun. Your flying glasses will keep the glare and reflection of the water from burning your eyes.

One of the cheapest kinds of insurance is the purchase of a good parachute and the know-how to use it.

Never forget to fly your craft every minute, right up to the second that you crash-land. If power is available, whether constant or intermittent, use it until just before contact is made with the ground or water. By doing so you can maneuver to the spot you wish to set down. If power has completely failed and you have sufficient elevation, nose down so that you have sufficient flying speed to sit down in the best spot you can find.

How to Ditch

If you are forced to ditch into the tops of heavy timber, make a slower than normal, flaps-down, nose-high glide heading uphill or level, if the terrain will permit.

Leave your landing gear up, if applicable—it will be a matter of judgment and the conditions you encounter at the time.

Never line up a tree or rock. Try to make your approach and landing as normal as possible in the treetops. Try to guide the airplane between the trees so that the wings will shear off and decelerate you rapidly.

If you are forced to set down in rocky terrain, make a slow, full-flap approach if you can. This will decelerate you rapidly and cut down on the danger of a head-on crash into the rocks.

Cut the switch just before landing.

Now that you are finally on the ground, toss your survival kit out and get away from the craft until you are certain all danger from fire is past.

Survival Techniques

Stay with your plane. Not only is the aircraft easier to spot from the air than a single person, but the plane can provide shelter. Parts of it can be used to provide reflectors, and materials from it can provide additional signals. So stay put, unless you are certain there will be no rescue efforts.

Check for injuries. Usually in the excitement of a forced landing in rough terrain you sustain some minor injuries you haven't been aware of. Treat all injuries immediately. (See the First Aid chapter.)

Anyone who comes through a crash landing he can walk away from is in some form of shock. Treat yourself for this condition first, before it becomes dangerous. Relax, then check your situation and decide what you can do about it.

Do not run around and wear yourself out. Conserve your energy. Plan a course of action. If you are lucky enough to land within walking distance of some sort of habitation, rest a short period before starting out.

If the aircraft has a radio that isn't too badly damaged, check it out and see if it is in working order. If it works, get on the emergency frequency to see if you can rouse anyone. If you can contact help, advise them of your physical condition, whether or not the plane can be salvaged and your location as near as you can ascertain. Also have them notify your family and friends that you are all right.

Signaling

If you don't have an aircraft radio transmitter, or if it is damaged beyond repair, get your signal equipment ready. (See the chapter on Signaling.) Gather plenty of dry wood and green limbs and leaves and make a smoky signal fire. In summer only one fire is necessary. Fire lookouts will spot it, and help will be on the way. In winter, when lookouts are not manned, build three fires about 50 feet apart. Any aircraft spotting this signal will know someone needs help.

If you can find a single evergreen tree in the open in a safe place, especially one with branches that reach to the ground, pile dry kindling and brush around its base and make a torch-tree out of it. Don't touch it off until you hear aircraft in the distance. Be sure to scrape a fire control line around its circumference and far enough away so that when the tree burns, it will fall within this safety line.

Use smoke, reflectors and light-colored cloth for daytime signals. At night use a flashlight, bright fires, signal flares or your landing lights if they are intact and operable.

If there is snow on the ground, tramp out huge S.O.S. letters. These should be as large as a cleared area will permit, at least 50 to 100 feet in size. Scrape and pile snow against one edge of the letters so that any sunlight will throw a shadow and assist in outlining the signal to better advantage.

In winter you will need warmth first, then shelter, and then food and water. In the desert in other hot areas a supply of water is first, then food and shelter. Keep off the ground and in the shade if possible. Otherwise, dig down 18 or 20 inches in the ground in the shade of a large rock or some brush. It will be from 20 to 40 percent cooler there.

If you have not been found and rescued within a week, the air search will probably be abandoned. But don't give up! Ground crews will generally continue the search off and on for a longer period, with air search continued at intervals.

If you finally decide that it is going to be a matter of a "walk-out," check your map for the easiest and shortest route to a place of habitation. Use your compass and map to direct your route. If your compass (either aircraft or pocket) is inoperative due to the crash, use the sun for general direction—remember it rises in the east and sets in the west! A few dazed survivors have forgotten this under stress. (See Chapters Two and Three.)

If you leave the crash scene, leave a note containing your name, physical condition, direction and place you are attempting to reach, and the time and date you left the area. This will help searchers in picking up your trail when they arrive at your "down-point."

RADIOTELEGRAPHIC CODE AND PHONETIC ALPHABET.

MAY DAY — — · — — · — — — · ·
                    · — — · — — Repeated at intervals.

SECURITY · · · · — · — ·
                  · · — — · — · · — — · — — Repeated.

PAN · — — · · — — · Repeated at intervals.

A	Alfa	·—		O	Oscar	———
B	Bravo	—···		P	Papa	·——·
C	Charlie	—·—·		Q	Quebec	——·—
D	Delta	—··		R	Romeo	·—·
E	Echo	·		S	Sierra	···
F	Foxtrot	··—·		T	Tango	—
G	Golf	——·		U	Uniform	··—
H	Hotel	····		V	Victor	···—
I	India	··		W	Whiskey	·——
J	Juliet	·———		X	Xray	—··—
K	Kilo	—·—		Y	Yankee	—·——
L	Lima	·—··		Z	Zulu	——··
M	Mike	——		SOS		···———···
N	November	—·				

If you hear voice or code Pan-Pan-Pan, it means an urgent message, or Security-Security-Security, it means a message concerning safety or a weather message—so stand by for the full text of the message.

Searches are expensive. They inconvenience other people, and the lives of other pilots have been sacrificed when searching for lost or overdue pilots. So file an arrival report immediately. Fly safely and have fun!

Aircraft Survival Kits

Survival Research Laboratories is recognized internationally as one of the world's leading designers of aircraft survival equipment. Their kits have been used successfully in all extremes of climate and terrain. The staff has collaborated with many outstanding survival specialists—bush pilots, explorers, medical authorities, Alaskan pilots and trappers, even military escape and evasion experts—who have added the benefit of their own personal experience and knowledge. Following are some of their recommendations. The list is fairly long, but the items are quite small, and the entire kit would easily fit into any plane.

CLOTHING

   a one-piece, R-1 (Army designation) lightweight
      suit
cold climate:
   knitted cap to cover ears
   two pairs socks, one heavy, one light
   extra gloves
Hot climate:
   broad-brimmed hat
   two pairs of light socks
Wet climate:
   plastic rain hat
   extra socks

FOOD

   two days rations as a minimum, in plastic containers
      rather than metal cans

EQUIPMENT

   fish hooks, strong line, leaders, sinkers and lures
   gill net
   snares or wire to make snares
   rifle and ammunition
   flashlight
   matches
   fire starters, candles
   liquid fuel stove and fuel (cold climates)
   solidified alcohol in cans or a liquid fuel stove (hot
      climates)
   compass
   maps

sleeping bag or jungle hammock
machete
Boy Scout knife
file
pliers
canteen with a water purification filter
two quarts of water
signal mirror
smoke signals
flare

MEDICAL EQUIPMENT

first aid kit
water purification tablets
toilet paper
insect repellent
anti-sunburn oil
sunglasses
snakebite kit

Aircraft flying over water should also include life vests and rafts. These should be packed separately from the survival kit. Sea marker dye, a signal mirror, a waterproof flashlight and shark repellent should also be included in the pack.

Index